THE RACE TO THE BOTTOM

A.A. Castor

Table of Contents

[The Race to the Bottom]
The OnlyFans Economy

A.A. CASTOR

A.A. Castor

A.A. Castor

Dedication

To my beloved family,

Your unconditional love, unwavering support, and endless encouragement have been my greatest blessings. From the earliest days of dreaming to the challenging moments of writing, you have stood by me with patience and belief. This book is as much yours as it is mine, a reflection of the values you've instilled and the faith you've shown in me. Thank you for being my rock and my inspiration.

To my dear friends,

Your friendship has illuminated my path with laughter, shared moments, and invaluable support. You've cheered me on through every triumph and lifted me up through every challenge. Your belief in my endeavors has been a source of strength and motivation. This book is a testament to the power of friendship, and I am grateful for each of you who has walked this journey by my side.

To God,

Your grace and guidance have been my constant companions. In moments of doubt, you've shown me the way; in moments of joy, you've multiplied my gratitude. This book is a testament to your faithfulness and the blessings you've bestowed upon me. May it serve as a reflection of your love and the lessons you continue to teach me.

With heartfelt gratitude and love,

A.A. Castor

Copyright © 2024 by A.A. Castor

Philippine Copyright Law:

Why I Am Writing This Book

The digital age has brought about profound changes in the way we interact, work, and express ourselves. Among the myriad of platforms that have emerged, OnlyFans stands out as one of the most influential and controversial. It has given rise to new forms of content creation, challenged traditional employment structures, and opened up discussions about privacy, ethics, and the commodification of personal and intimate aspects of life. Yet, despite its significant impact, the deeper implications of OnlyFans on society, culture, and the economy are often overlooked or misunderstood.

I am writing this book to shed light on these complexities, to explore the nuanced realities that both creators and subscribers face in this new digital landscape. My goal is to provide a comprehensive analysis of OnlyFans, not just as a platform, but as a cultural phenomenon that reflects and influences broader societal trends.

Personal Motivation

My interest in writing this book stems from a deep curiosity about the intersections of technology, culture, and human behavior. As someone who has closely observed the rise of digital platforms over the years, I have seen how they can empower individuals, democratize access to opportunities, and foster creativity. However, I have also witnessed the challenges and ethical dilemmas that come with these innovations. OnlyFans, in particular, encapsulates these dualities in a way that is both compelling and concerning.

This book is not just an academic exploration; it is a personal journey into understanding how digital platforms like OnlyFans are reshaping our lives. I want to understand the motivations, aspirations, and struggles of the people who use this platform—both creators and subscribers. By diving into their stories, I hope to present a balanced and empathetic view of the opportunities and risks associated with this new form of digital interaction.

A Call for Dialogue

One of the primary reasons I am writing this book is to spark a broader conversation about the ethical and cultural implications of platforms like OnlyFans. Too often, discussions about digital content creation are polarized, with voices either celebrating the empowerment of creators or condemning the platform for its perceived moral shortcomings. I believe the truth lies somewhere in between, and it is through thoughtful dialogue that we can begin to navigate these complexities.

This book aims to be a starting point for such conversations, encouraging readers to think critically about the role of digital platforms in their own lives and in society at large. It is an invitation to question, reflect, and engage with the issues at hand, rather than accepting them at face value.

Exploring the Moral Dimensions

Another key motivation for writing this book is to delve into the moral dimensions of OnlyFans and its impact on individuals and society. The platform raises important questions about the commodification of intimacy, the ethics of digital labor, and the ways in which we define and value work in the modern economy. These are not easy questions, and there are no simple answers. However, by exploring these issues in depth, I hope to provide a framework for understanding the moral complexities involved and to offer insights that can guide ethical decision-making in this evolving landscape.

Looking Toward the Future

Finally, I am writing this book with an eye toward the future. The rapid pace of technological change means that platforms like OnlyFans will continue to evolve, and new challenges and opportunities will emerge. By examining the current state of the platform and its broader implications, I aim to provide readers with the tools they need to navigate the future of digital content creation with awareness and intention.

I also want to highlight the potential for positive change—how platforms like OnlyFans can be leveraged to promote inclusivity, support marginalized voices, and create new economic opportunities for those who need them most. By addressing the challenges and seizing the opportunities, we can help shape a digital future that is more ethical, equitable, and empowering for all.

Conclusion

In writing this book, my intention is to explore the multifaceted impact of OnlyFans on our society, our economy, and our personal lives. I hope to provide a nuanced perspective that recognizes both the empowering potential of the platform and the ethical dilemmas it presents. Ultimately, this book is an invitation to engage in a thoughtful and informed discussion about the future of digital content creation, the role of platforms like OnlyFans, and the values that will guide us in this new era.

Thank you for joining me on this journey. I hope that this book will inspire you to think more deeply about the digital world we are creating and the choices we make within it.

Warning and Disclaimer

The content presented in this book is intended for informational and educational purposes only. While every effort has been made to ensure the accuracy and reliability of the information provided, the author and publisher make no representations or warranties of any kind, express or implied, regarding the completeness, accuracy, or suitability of the content contained herein.

Content and Ethical Considerations

The topics discussed in this book, particularly those related to OnlyFans and digital content creation, may involve sensitive or controversial subject matter, including discussions about adult content, digital labor, and ethical dilemmas. Readers are advised to approach these topics with an open mind and a critical perspective. The views and opinions expressed in this book are those of the author and do not necessarily reflect the official policy or position of any organization or platform discussed.

This book is not intended to endorse or criticize any specific platform, content creator, or subscriber behavior. Rather, it aims to provide a balanced analysis of the opportunities, challenges, and ethical considerations associated with digital content creation on platforms like OnlyFans.

Legal Disclaimer

The author and publisher are not liable for any direct, indirect, incidental, or consequential damages that may result from the use or application of the information contained in this book. Readers are advised to seek professional legal, financial, or psychological advice if they are considering engaging with platforms like OnlyFans, whether as content creators or subscribers.

Tax and Legal Advice: Any discussion of legal or tax matters is for general informational purposes only and should not be relied upon as legal or tax advice. Laws and regulations governing digital content creation, taxation, and platform usage vary by jurisdiction and are subject to change. Readers should consult with a qualified legal or tax professional to address their specific needs and circumstances.

Mental Health and Well-being: The book touches on mental health issues related to digital content creation and online interactions. While resources and suggestions are provided, they are not a substitute for professional mental health care. Individuals experiencing mental health challenges should seek the assistance of a licensed mental health professional.

Responsibility of the Reader

By reading this book, you acknowledge that you understand the potential risks and challenges associated with digital content creation and the use of platforms like OnlyFans. You agree that you are responsible for your own decisions and actions, and you will not hold the author or publisher liable for any consequences that may arise from applying the information provided in this book.

Future Developments

The digital landscape is continually evolving, and the platforms, policies, and societal norms discussed in this book may change over time. The author and publisher do not guarantee that the information presented will remain current or applicable in the future. Readers are encouraged to stay informed about developments in digital content creation and platform policies to make well-informed decisions.

Conclusion

This book is intended to foster a deeper understanding of the complex issues surrounding digital content creation and the use of platforms like OnlyFans. While the information provided is intended to be helpful and informative, it is ultimately the responsibility of the reader to apply this knowledge thoughtfully and ethically in their own lives. The author and publisher hope that this book will serve as a valuable resource for navigating the evolving digital landscape with awareness, integrity, and responsibility.

Thank you for your understanding.
     Mr. A.A. Castor

About the Author

A.A. Castor is a seasoned writer, researcher, and digital media expert with a deep interest in the intersection of technology, culture, and society. With a background in media studies and sociology, A.A. Castor has spent years exploring how digital platforms are reshaping the way we live, work, and connect with each other.

Over the course of their career, A.A. Castor has authored several articles, reports, and books on topics ranging from the gig economy and digital content creation to the ethical implications of emerging technologies. Their work is known for its balanced and nuanced approach, offering readers a comprehensive understanding of the complexities involved in the digital age.

In addition to writing, A.A. Castor has served as a consultant and speaker for various organizations, helping them navigate the challenges and opportunities presented by digital transformation. Their insights are regularly sought by media outlets, academic institutions, and industry leaders who are grappling with the rapid changes in digital media and content creation.

A.A. Castor is passionate about fostering thoughtful dialogue on the ethical and societal implications of digital platforms. They believe that as technology continues to evolve, it is crucial to engage in conversations that prioritize human dignity, inclusivity, and ethical responsibility. Through their work, A.A. Castor aims to provide readers with the tools and insights needed to navigate the complexities of the digital age with awareness and integrity.

1. Introduction to the OnlyFans Economy

Overview of OnlyFans as a Platform

History and Development of OnlyFans

Founding and Early Days:

OnlyFans was launched in 2016 by British entrepreneur Tim Stokely, who had a history of developing platforms aimed at monetizing adult content. Stokely's earlier ventures, including a site called GlamWorship, laid the groundwork for what would become OnlyFans. The idea behind OnlyFans was to create a platform where content creators could offer exclusive content directly to their audience in exchange for a subscription fee. This model was designed to empower creators by giving them a direct income stream from their most dedicated fans.

Initially, OnlyFans was a niche platform, attracting a variety of content creators from fitness trainers to artists who saw it as a way to monetize their content without relying on traditional ad revenue models. It provided an opportunity for creators to have more control over their income, bypassing traditional media and advertising channels. In the early days, the platform's user base was relatively small, and it was seen as one of many platforms offering similar services.

Growth and Popularity:

OnlyFans experienced steady growth in its first few years, but it was the COVID-19 pandemic in 2020 that truly catapulted the platform into the mainstream. As lockdowns around the world disrupted traditional forms of income, particularly for those in the entertainment and service industries, many individuals turned to OnlyFans as a new source of revenue. The platform's model of direct-to-consumer sales became highly attractive during a time when personal interactions and performances were severely limited.

The pandemic also accelerated the platform's association with adult content. While OnlyFans had initially attracted a diverse group of creators, the flexibility of the platform quickly made it popular among sex workers and adult entertainers. These creators found OnlyFans to be a safer and more profitable alternative to traditional methods of income generation in the adult industry, where exploitation and intermediaries often took a significant cut of earnings.

By 2021, OnlyFans had over 120 million registered users and more than 2 million content creators. The platform had become a cultural phenomenon, regularly featured in mainstream media and discussed across various social platforms. Celebrities and influencers also began to join OnlyFans, either to share exclusive content with their fans or to take advantage of the platform's lucrative earning potential. This influx of high-profile users further drove the platform's visibility and growth.

Notable Milestones:

One of the most significant events in OnlyFans' history occurred in August 2021, when the platform announced that it would ban sexually explicit content. This decision was met with immediate backlash from the creator community, as well as from advocates for sex workers, who viewed the move as a betrayal of the platform's core user base. The decision was reportedly driven by pressure from financial institutions and payment processors, which were concerned about the legal and reputational risks associated with adult content.

However, within a week, OnlyFans reversed this decision after facing immense criticism from both creators and subscribers. The incident highlighted the platform's dependency on adult content and the challenges it faces in navigating the regulatory and financial landscape. Despite the reversal, the event sparked a broader discussion about the future of content on OnlyFans and the risks of platforms de-platforming creators.

As of 2024, OnlyFans continues to be a dominant force in the online content subscription market, with ongoing discussions about its impact on the digital economy, creator empowerment, and the ethics of content monetization.

Key Features and Functionalities

Subscription Model:

The core of OnlyFans' business model is its subscription service. Creators can set a monthly subscription fee, which their fans (subscribers) must pay to access their content. This subscription model is highly flexible, allowing creators to price their content based on the perceived value and exclusivity. Subscriptions typically range from as low as $4.99 to upwards of $49.99 per month, though some high-profile creators charge even more.

Subscribers gain access to a creator's content as long as they maintain their subscription. This content can include photos, videos, and written posts. The subscription model incentivizes creators to produce regular, high-quality content to retain subscribers and reduce churn rates. Unlike platforms that rely on ad revenue, OnlyFans' subscription model creates a direct financial relationship between creators and their audience, giving creators a steady, predictable income stream.

Pay-Per-View (PPV) Content:

In addition to the monthly subscription, creators can offer Pay-Per-View (PPV) content. This allows them to charge extra for specific pieces of content, such as exclusive videos or photos. PPV content can be sent directly to subscribers through messages or posted on the creator's feed with a price tag. This feature enables creators to monetize their most premium content further and provides an additional revenue stream beyond the subscription.

PPV content is particularly popular among creators who offer personalized or custom content, as it allows them to cater to specific requests from fans willing to pay a premium for tailored experiences. This functionality has become a key component of the platform, especially for creators in the adult entertainment industry, where personalized content can command high prices.

Direct Messaging:

One of the standout features of OnlyFans is the direct messaging system, which allows creators to interact personally with their subscribers. This feature has been instrumental in building parasocial relationships between creators and their fans, making the platform more engaging and lucrative. Creators can use direct messaging to build closer connections with their fans, offering them personalized interactions that go beyond what is available on public social media platforms.

Direct messaging also serves as a significant revenue source, as creators can charge for one-on-one chats, personalized content, and exclusive insights. For instance, a fan might pay for a private message containing a custom video or photo, or simply to have a conversation with their favorite creator. This level of interaction has proven to be highly profitable, as it taps into the fan's desire for a personal connection with the creator.

Tipping:

OnlyFans incorporates a tipping feature, allowing subscribers to give creators additional money as a token of appreciation or in exchange for specific content or actions. Tipping can occur during live streams, in direct messages, or through regular posts. The tipping feature is versatile, enabling fans to support creators beyond their subscription payments and encouraging creators to engage more with their audience.

Tipping is particularly popular during live streams, where fans can tip in real-time to show support or make requests. This feature not only increases the earnings potential for creators but also fosters a sense of community and interaction between creators and their subscribers. Creators often incentivize tipping by offering shout-outs, personalized responses, or exclusive content in return.

Content Flexibility:

OnlyFans provides creators with a high degree of flexibility regarding the types of content they can offer. Creators can upload photos, videos, and written posts, host live streams, and offer PPV content. This flexibility allows creators to tailor their content strategies to what works best for them and their audience. Some creators focus on daily photo updates, while others may produce long-form videos or engage in regular live streams.

The platform's flexibility also extends to how creators manage their content. They can schedule posts in advance, use the platform's built-in analytics to track performance, and adjust their content strategies based on subscriber feedback and engagement metrics. This adaptability has made OnlyFans appealing to a wide range of creators, from fitness trainers offering workout routines to adult entertainers producing explicit content.

Monetization Control:

OnlyFans is built on the principle of giving creators full control over their monetization strategies. Creators can set their subscription rates, choose whether to offer PPV content, decide how much to charge for direct messages, and even accept tips. This control over pricing and content allows creators to experiment with different monetization strategies to find what works best for their audience.

Creators also have the flexibility to offer discounts, free trials, and bundles to attract and retain subscribers. OnlyFans' backend provides tools for creators to analyze their income streams, track subscriber trends, and optimize their offerings. This level of control over monetization is one of the platform's most significant draws, as it allows creators to maximize their earnings while maintaining creative freedom.

Comparison with Other Subscription-Based Platforms

Patreon:

Patreon is a popular subscription platform that predates OnlyFans, having been founded in 2013. Like OnlyFans, Patreon allows creators to offer exclusive content to subscribers for a monthly fee. However, Patreon is more diverse in the types of content it supports, catering to creators from various fields, including musicians, writers, podcasters, and visual artists.

Patreon offers a tiered subscription model, where creators can set multiple pricing levels, each offering different levels of access or perks. For example, a musician might offer behind-the-scenes content at a lower tier, while providing early access to new releases at a higher tier. Unlike OnlyFans, Patreon is more restrictive regarding adult content, which limits its appeal to creators in the adult entertainment industry.

Patreon also focuses heavily on community building, offering tools for creators to interact with their fans through posts, comments, and private messages. However, its user interface and feature set are generally considered more complex than OnlyFans, which has a more straightforward, user-friendly approach.

Ko-fi:

Ko-fi is another platform that allows creators to monetize their content through fan support. Unlike OnlyFans and Patreon, Ko-fi started as a way for creators to receive small, one-time donations from their fans, typically represented as "buying a coffee." Over time, Ko-fi has evolved to include monthly memberships, similar to Patreon and OnlyFans.

Ko-fi is less focused on exclusive content and more on enabling creators to receive financial support for their work, regardless of the medium. The platform does not take a cut of the donations or subscriptions, which can be appealing to creators who want to maximize their earnings. However, Ko-fi lacks the robust content delivery and interaction features of OnlyFans, making it more suitable for creators who are already established on other platforms and are looking for an additional income stream.

Ko-fi's simplicity is both its strength and limitation. It is easy to use and set up, but it does not offer the comprehensive content management and monetization tools found on OnlyFans or Patreon.

Substack:

Substack is a subscription-based platform focused on writers and journalists, allowing them to monetize newsletters. Launched in 2017, Substack has become a popular platform for independent writers looking to build a direct relationship with their readers. Unlike OnlyFans, which is heavily visual and interactive, Substack is text-focused, catering to an audience interested in in-depth analysis, commentary, and journalism.

Substack's revenue model is straightforward: writers can offer free content or charge a subscription fee for access to premium newsletters. Substack takes a 10% cut of subscription revenue, allowing writers to retain the majority of their earnings. The platform has gained traction among journalists who have left traditional media outlets to start their own independent publications.

While Substack excels in its niche, it does not offer the diverse content options or interactive features available on OnlyFans. Its focus on written content also means it attracts a different type of creator and audience, one more interested in reading and less in visual or interactive content.

Twitch:

Twitch is primarily known as a live-streaming platform, particularly popular in the gaming community. However, it also offers a subscription model where viewers can support their favorite streamers through monthly payments. Unlike OnlyFans, Twitch is focused on live content, with streamers often broadcasting for hours at a time, engaging with their audience in real-time.

Twitch streamers can earn money through subscriptions, ad revenue, donations, and sponsorships. Twitch's revenue model is more diverse than OnlyFans, with streamers often relying on a combination of these income streams. The platform also supports tiered subscriptions, where viewers can pay more for additional perks, such as exclusive emotes or ad-free viewing.

Twitch's audience is more niche, primarily consisting of gamers and eSports fans, though it has expanded to include categories like music, cooking, and just chatting. While Twitch's focus on live content differentiates it from OnlyFans, the two platforms share similarities in their reliance on direct fan support and interactive features.

Comparison Summary:

OnlyFans stands out in the subscription-based platform market for its robust monetization options, direct interaction capabilities, and flexibility in content types. While other platforms like Patreon and Substack offer subscription models, OnlyFans is unique in its appeal to adult content creators and those seeking direct, monetizable engagement with their audience. Its user-friendly interface, combined with extensive monetization control, makes it an attractive option for creators who want to maintain full control over their content and earnings.

In contrast, platforms like Patreon and Substack cater to broader or more niche audiences, with features and policies that reflect their specific target markets. Ko-fi and Twitch offer alternatives for creators looking for simpler or more live-focused monetization options, but they lack the comprehensive content management and monetization tools that OnlyFans provides.

This detailed overview highlights how OnlyFans has carved out a significant niche in the digital content economy, offering features and functionalities that cater to a wide range of creators while maintaining a particular appeal for those in the adult entertainment industry.

Growth and Popularity Trends of OnlyFans

Statistical Analysis of User Growth

Initial Growth and Market Penetration (2016-2018):

In its early years, OnlyFans grew slowly but steadily. The platform's initial growth phase was driven by word-of-mouth among niche communities, including fitness trainers, models, and small-scale influencers who saw the platform as a way to monetize their content without relying on traditional advertising models. During this period, the platform had a relatively modest user base, with around 100,000 users by the end of 2017. The user growth was organic, with minimal marketing efforts, as the platform largely relied on the appeal of direct monetization to attract creators.

Emergence as a Platform for Adult Content (2018-2019):

By 2018, OnlyFans began to gain traction as a platform for adult content creators. This shift was not part of an official rebranding but rather a natural evolution driven by the platform's features that allowed for direct and private content sharing, combined with the subscription model that guaranteed steady income for creators. The ease with which creators could set up accounts and monetize explicit content attracted a significant number of adult entertainers who were looking for a safer and more profitable alternative to traditional avenues like camming sites or in-person work.

During this period, the platform's growth began to accelerate. By mid-2019, OnlyFans had approximately 7 million registered users and over 60,000 content creators. The growth was fueled by the increasing visibility of the platform in online communities and the growing acceptance of adult content as a legitimate form of digital entrepreneurship.

Pandemic-Induced Surge (2020):

The COVID-19 pandemic marked a turning point in the growth trajectory of OnlyFans. As lockdowns and social distancing measures were implemented worldwide, many individuals, particularly those in the service, entertainment, and sex work industries, found themselves out of work or with reduced income. OnlyFans provided an accessible and immediate way for these individuals to generate income by leveraging their existing social media followings or creating new content.

The platform saw a dramatic increase in both user registrations and active creators during this time. By May 2020, the number of users had surged to 30 million, and the platform had over 450,000 content creators. This represented a more than fourfold increase in user base in just a few months. The surge was largely driven by the platform's ability to provide economic opportunities during a time of global financial uncertainty.

The pandemic also led to increased media coverage of OnlyFans, both positive and negative. Articles and news segments highlighted the platform's role in the growing gig economy, with some praising it as an empowering tool for creators, while others criticized it for contributing to the commodification of personal content, particularly in the adult entertainment sector.

Exponential Growth and Cultural Mainstreaming (2020-2021):

Following the initial surge in early 2020, OnlyFans continued to experience exponential growth. By December 2020, the platform boasted over 90 million registered users and 1 million content creators. This growth was driven by several factors, including the platform's increasing cultural relevance, the entry of celebrities into the space, and the broadening of content offerings beyond strictly adult content.

Celebrities and influencers like Bella Thorne, Cardi B, and Tyga joined OnlyFans, bringing mainstream attention and a wave of new users. Bella Thorne's entry into the platform was particularly notable;

she claimed to have earned over $1 million within 24 hours of joining. However, her presence also sparked controversy among existing creators, particularly after her actions led to policy changes on the platform that affected all creators. These changes included caps on tips and pay-per-view pricing, which were implemented after Thorne's subscribers requested refunds for content they felt did not meet their expectations.

This period also saw the normalization of OnlyFans within popular culture, with references to the platform appearing in music, television, and social media. The term "OnlyFans" became synonymous with direct-to-consumer content monetization, particularly within the adult content sphere, but also in other areas like fitness, cooking, and influencer marketing.

Challenges and Controversies (2021):

The rapid growth of OnlyFans was not without its challenges. In August 2021, the platform announced a policy change that would ban sexually explicit content, a decision driven by pressure from financial institutions and payment processors concerned about the platform's association with adult content. The announcement sparked immediate backlash from creators and users alike, leading to widespread criticism of the platform's decision to distance itself from the very content that had driven its growth.

Within a week, OnlyFans reversed the decision, citing the outcry from its community and a renewed commitment to supporting all types of content creators. The incident highlighted the platform's dependence on adult content and the delicate balance it needed to maintain between regulatory compliance and creator autonomy. The controversy also led to increased scrutiny from regulators, media, and advocacy groups regarding the platform's policies and the potential exploitation of content creators.

Despite the reversal, the incident caused lasting damage to the platform's reputation among some creators, leading to a migration of users to alternative platforms like Fansly and JustForFans. However, the platform's user base continued to grow, albeit at a slower rate, with over 130 million registered users by the end of 2021.

Consolidation and Diversification (2022-2024):

In the years following the 2021 controversy, OnlyFans focused on consolidating its user base and diversifying its content offerings. The platform introduced new features aimed at enhancing user experience, such as advanced analytics tools for creators, enhanced security measures for subscribers, and more robust content management systems. These developments were part of an effort to attract a broader range of creators from industries like education, music, and fitness, while still maintaining its core user base in the adult content market.

By 2024, OnlyFans had over 200 million registered users and more than 2.5 million content creators. The platform's growth had stabilized, with continued expansion into new markets and demographics. OnlyFans also began exploring partnerships with mainstream media companies and content creators, further broadening its appeal and attempting to rebrand itself as a more inclusive platform for all types of creators.

However, the platform's association with adult content remains strong, and this continues to be both a driving force for its success and a challenge in terms of public perception and regulatory scrutiny. The platform's efforts to diversify content offerings have had mixed results, with some non-adult content creators finding success, while others struggle to gain traction in an ecosystem still dominated by explicit material.

Demographics of Creators and Subscribers

Creators:

The creator demographic on OnlyFans is diverse but heavily skewed towards younger adults, particularly those aged 18-35. The platform is popular among individuals from a variety of backgrounds, including traditional sex workers, social media influencers, fitness trainers, musicians, and models. However, it is the adult content creators who make up the majority of the platform's most successful users.

Gender Distribution:

Women represent the majority of content creators on OnlyFans, particularly in the adult content category. The platform has been especially empowering for women who can control their content and earnings without relying on third-party agencies or platforms that take significant cuts. However, there is also a growing number of male creators, particularly in the fitness and LGBTQ+ niches, who are finding success on the platform.

Geographic Distribution:

The majority of creators on OnlyFans are based in North America and Europe, reflecting the platform's strongest markets. However, there is a growing presence of creators from Latin America, Asia, and Australia. The platform's global reach allows creators from different regions to tap into international audiences, expanding their potential subscriber base beyond their local markets.

Economic Backgrounds:

OnlyFans has attracted creators from various economic backgrounds, including those from disadvantaged or marginalized communities. The platform's low barrier to entry and potential for high earnings have made it an attractive option for individuals who may face barriers to entry in traditional industries. However, the platform's success can vary widely, with a small percentage of creators earning the majority of the income, while many others struggle to gain visibility and subscribers.

Motivations and Content Strategies:

Creators on OnlyFans are motivated by a range of factors, from financial necessity to the desire for creative freedom. Many creators are drawn to the platform for its ability to provide a steady income stream, particularly in the adult content space where traditional avenues may be less profitable or safe. Others see OnlyFans as a way to build a personal brand, leveraging the platform's tools to engage directly with their audience.

Content strategies on OnlyFans vary widely depending on the creator's niche. Adult content creators often focus on explicit material, offering a mix of photos, videos, and live streams. Fitness and lifestyle creators may offer workout routines, diet plans, and personal coaching sessions. Musicians and artists might use the platform to share exclusive tracks, behind-the-scenes content, or live performances. The diversity of content on OnlyFans is one of its strengths, allowing creators to tailor their offerings to their specific audience and monetize their unique talents.

Subscribers:

The subscriber demographic on OnlyFans is predominantly male, with a large proportion falling within the 25-44 age range. Subscribers are drawn to OnlyFans for the opportunity to access exclusive content and interact directly with their favorite creators. The appeal of personalized content and the ability to engage one-on-one with creators are significant factors driving subscription and tipping behavior on the platform.

Gender and Age Distribution:

While the majority of subscribers are male, the platform also has a significant number of female users, particularly in niches such as fitness, cooking, and lifestyle. The age distribution skews towards younger adults, with the largest group being those aged 25-34, followed by those aged 35-44. This demographic is often characterized by disposable income and a familiarity with digital platforms, making them prime candidates for subscription services like OnlyFans.

Geographic Distribution:

Subscribers on OnlyFans are primarily based in North America and Europe, but the platform's reach is global. As the platform has expanded, it has attracted subscribers from various regions, including Latin America, Asia, and Australia. The global nature of OnlyFans allows creators to tap into diverse markets, and subscribers can access content from creators worldwide, often drawn by niche interests or unique content offerings.

Motivations and Spending Behavior:

Subscribers are motivated by the desire for exclusive, often personalized content that they cannot find elsewhere. The platform's model of direct interaction between creators and subscribers fosters a sense of intimacy and loyalty, encouraging subscribers to maintain their subscriptions over time. Many subscribers are willing to pay a premium for personalized interactions, custom content, and the ability to support their favorite creators directly.

Spending behavior on OnlyFans is characterized by a combination of subscription fees, tips, and pay-per-view purchases. Subscribers who feel a strong connection with a creator are often more likely to engage in tipping or purchasing additional content. The platform's monetization features, such as private messaging and custom content requests, further enhance the spending potential of subscribers, making it a lucrative environment for creators who can effectively engage their audience.

Economic Impact on Subscribers:

The economic impact of OnlyFans on subscribers varies. For some, the platform represents a significant portion of their discretionary spending, with individuals allocating a portion of their monthly budget to support their favorite creators. For others, particularly those in lower income brackets, spending on OnlyFans can lead to financial strain, especially if the platform's addictive nature encourages excessive spending. The platform's direct payment model, combined with the personal connection subscribers feel with creators, can sometimes result in higher overall spending than traditional subscription services.

Major Milestones and Turning Points in the Platform's History

Launch and Early Growth (2016-2018):

OnlyFans was launched in 2016 by British entrepreneur Tim Stokely. The platform was designed to provide content creators with a direct way to monetize their content by offering it to fans through a subscription model. In its early years, OnlyFans grew slowly but steadily, largely through word-of-mouth among niche communities. The platform attracted a diverse range of creators, including fitness trainers, musicians, and small-scale influencers who saw the platform as a way to earn income without relying on traditional advertising models.

During this period, OnlyFans had a relatively small user base but gained traction among creators looking for an alternative to ad-based revenue models. The platform's initial success was driven by its promise of financial independence for creators and its straightforward, user-friendly interface that allowed anyone to set up an account and start earning.

Emergence of Adult Content as a Core Offering (2018-2019):

By 2018, OnlyFans began to gain significant traction as a platform for adult content. This shift was not an official rebranding but rather a natural evolution driven by the platform's features, which allowed for private, direct-to-consumer content sharing. The subscription model, combined with the ability to offer personalized content through direct messaging and pay-per-view options, made OnlyFans particularly appealing to adult content creators.

As more adult entertainers joined the platform, OnlyFans' user base grew rapidly. By mid-2019, the platform had around 7 million registered users and over 60,000 content creators. This growth marked a turning point for OnlyFans, as it began to gain a reputation as a go-to platform for adult content, despite hosting creators from a wide range of industries.

Celebrity Involvement and Mainstream Attention (2019-2020):

The platform's growth was further accelerated by the involvement of celebrities and mainstream influencers in 2019 and 2020. High-profile figures like Cardi B, Bella Thorne, and Tyga joined OnlyFans, bringing significant media attention and millions of new users to the platform. Bella Thorne's entry into the platform was particularly notable; she made headlines for earning over $1 million within 24 hours of joining. However, her presence also sparked controversy among existing creators, particularly after her actions led to changes in the platform's tipping and pay-per-view policies.

The involvement of celebrities helped to normalize OnlyFans within popular culture, positioning it as a legitimate platform for content creators of all types. However, it also highlighted tensions between traditional celebrities and grassroots creators who had built the platform's early success. The influx of high-profile users brought new opportunities for monetization but also led to increased scrutiny from the media and public.

Pandemic Surge and Cultural Impact (2020):

The COVID-19 pandemic was a watershed moment for OnlyFans. With global lockdowns and economic uncertainty, many individuals turned to the platform as a way to generate income. OnlyFans provided an accessible and immediate way for people, particularly those in the service and entertainment industries, to monetize their content and connect with audiences in a time of social distancing.

The pandemic-induced surge led to a massive increase in user registrations and active creators. By May 2020, OnlyFans had over 30 million registered users and 450,000 content creators, marking an exponential growth from the previous year. The platform's role in the gig economy during this period was widely covered in the media, with stories highlighting its impact on digital entrepreneurship and the adult content industry.

The pandemic also accelerated OnlyFans' integration into mainstream culture. The platform was frequently referenced in music, television, and social media, becoming synonymous with direct-to-consumer content monetization. This period solidified OnlyFans as a major player in the digital economy, particularly within the adult content space.

Controversy and Policy Reversal (2021):

In August 2021, OnlyFans faced one of its most significant challenges when it announced a ban on sexually explicit content. The decision, driven by pressure from financial institutions and payment processors, sparked immediate backlash from creators and users. Many viewed the decision as a betrayal of the platform's core user base, as adult content creators had been instrumental in driving OnlyFans' growth.

The backlash was swift and widespread, with creators and advocates criticizing the platform for abandoning the community that had built its success. Within a week, OnlyFans reversed the decision, announcing that it would continue to allow adult content on the platform. The incident highlighted the platform's dependence on adult content and the challenges of balancing regulatory compliance with creator autonomy.

The controversy also led to increased scrutiny from regulators, media, and advocacy groups regarding the platform's policies and the potential exploitation of content creators. Despite the reversal, the incident caused lasting damage to the platform's reputation among some creators, leading to a migration of users to alternative platforms like Fansly and JustForFans. However, the platform's user base continued to grow, albeit at a slower rate, with over 130 million registered users by the end of 2021.

Consolidation, Diversification, and Future Prospects (2022-2024):

Following the 2021 controversy, OnlyFans focused on consolidating its user base and diversifying its content offerings. The platform introduced new features aimed at enhancing user experience, such as advanced analytics tools for creators, enhanced security measures for subscribers, and more robust content management systems. These developments were part of an effort to attract a broader range of creators from industries like education, music, and fitness, while still maintaining its core user base in the adult content market.

By 2024, OnlyFans had over 200 million registered users and more than 2.5 million content creators. The platform's growth had stabilized, with continued expansion into new markets and demographics. OnlyFans also began exploring partnerships with mainstream media companies and content creators, further broadening its appeal and attempting to rebrand itself as a more inclusive platform for all types of creators.

However, the platform's association with adult content remains strong, and this continues to be both a driving force for its success and a challenge in terms of public perception and regulatory scrutiny. The platform's efforts to diversify content offerings have had mixed results, with some non-adult content creators finding success, while others struggle to gain traction in an ecosystem still dominated by explicit material.

Looking forward, OnlyFans faces both opportunities and challenges. The platform's ability to innovate and adapt to changing market conditions will be crucial in maintaining its position as a leader in the digital content subscription industry. As regulatory pressures and public scrutiny continue to mount, OnlyFans will need to navigate the complex landscape of content moderation, creator support, and consumer demand to sustain its growth and relevance in the years to come.

Societal and Economic Impact of OnlyFans

Influence on the Gig Economy

Redefining Digital Entrepreneurship:
OnlyFans has played a pivotal role in redefining digital entrepreneurship, particularly within the gig economy. Traditionally, the gig economy has been dominated by platforms like Uber, Airbnb, and TaskRabbit, where workers perform physical or service-based tasks. However, OnlyFans has expanded the scope of the gig economy to include digital content creation, where individuals can monetize their personal brand and content directly from their audience.

Unlike other gig platforms that often involve intermediary companies taking a significant portion of the earnings, OnlyFans allows creators to retain a much larger share of their income. Creators can set their own prices, control their content, and interact directly with their subscribers, providing a level of autonomy and financial control that is uncommon in other areas of the gig economy.

Economic Empowerment for Creators:
For many creators, OnlyFans has provided a significant source of income, particularly during times of economic uncertainty, such as the COVID-19 pandemic. The platform has empowered individuals, especially women and marginalized communities, to earn a living on their own terms. This empowerment has been especially important for those who have faced barriers to entry in traditional employment or who have been economically disadvantaged due to systemic issues.

The financial success of some creators on OnlyFans has highlighted the potential for substantial earnings in the digital content space. High-profile creators, including those in the adult entertainment industry, have reported earning thousands, if not millions, of dollars monthly. This level of income has been a game-changer for many, allowing them to achieve financial independence and, in some cases, build significant personal wealth.

Challenges and Risks in the Gig Economy Context:

Despite its potential for economic empowerment, OnlyFans also presents challenges and risks typical of the gig economy. Income on the platform can be highly variable, with many creators struggling to gain visibility and build a substantial subscriber base. The top earners on OnlyFans represent a small percentage of the overall creator population, with a vast majority earning modest sums. This income inequality mirrors broader trends in the gig economy, where a small number of workers capture the majority of the earnings.

Moreover, creators on OnlyFans are responsible for all aspects of their business, from content creation to marketing to customer service. This level of responsibility can be overwhelming, particularly for those who are new to digital entrepreneurship. The lack of traditional job benefits, such as health insurance, retirement plans, and job security, also places creators at financial risk, especially in the event of a downturn in their subscriber base or changes in platform policies.

Regulatory and Taxation Implications:

As OnlyFans has grown, it has attracted the attention of regulators and tax authorities. Creators on the platform are considered self-employed, which means they are responsible for reporting their income and paying taxes on their earnings. However, the complex nature of digital income and the global reach of the platform can create challenges in ensuring compliance with tax regulations. This has led to calls for clearer guidelines and support for digital workers in navigating the tax landscape.

Regulation of the platform itself has also become a point of debate, particularly regarding the hosting of adult content and the responsibilities of platforms in moderating and policing content. OnlyFans has had to navigate these regulatory challenges carefully to maintain its business model while adhering to legal requirements in different jurisdictions.

Shifts in Traditional Employment Paradigms

Erosion of Traditional Employment Structures:

The rise of OnlyFans and similar platforms has contributed to a broader shift away from traditional employment structures towards more flexible, freelance-based work. For many individuals, the ability to earn money online, directly from their audience, has made traditional 9-to-5 jobs less appealing. This shift has been particularly pronounced among younger generations, who value flexibility, autonomy, and the ability to pursue creative passions over the stability of traditional employment.

OnlyFans has exemplified this shift by providing a platform where individuals can monetize their personal brand and content without the need for an employer or intermediary. This model of work challenges traditional employment paradigms, where income is typically tied to a set salary, fixed hours, and the hierarchical structure of a company. On OnlyFans, creators have the freedom to set their schedules, choose their content, and directly engage with their audience, creating a more dynamic and personalized work environment.

Impact on the Creative Industry:

The platform has also had a significant impact on the creative industry, where traditional gatekeepers, such as record labels, publishers, and galleries, have historically controlled access to audiences and income. OnlyFans has democratized the ability to earn money from creative work, allowing creators to bypass these gatekeepers and retain full control over their content and earnings. This shift has been particularly empowering for independent creators, who have struggled to gain recognition or financial success through traditional channels.

However, the success of OnlyFans has also sparked debates within the creative industry about the value of content and the ethics of monetizing personal and often explicit material. Critics argue that the platform commodifies personal and intimate aspects of creators' lives, potentially leading to exploitation and the erosion of traditional artistic and ethical standards. Supporters, on the other hand, view OnlyFans as a platform that empowers creators to take control of their careers and earn a living on their terms.

Repercussions for Traditional Employment Sectors:

The success of OnlyFans has had ripple effects across various traditional employment sectors, particularly those related to entertainment, media, and adult services. For example, the adult entertainment industry has seen a shift as performers increasingly turn to OnlyFans to generate income independently, rather than relying on studios, agencies, or other intermediaries. This shift has disrupted traditional business models within the industry and has led to changes in how adult content is produced, distributed, and consumed.

In the broader entertainment and media landscape, OnlyFans has highlighted the potential for direct-to-consumer monetization, prompting other platforms and industries to explore similar models. For instance, musicians, actors, and influencers are increasingly looking for ways to monetize their content directly, bypassing traditional distribution channels and intermediaries.

This shift towards direct monetization and the gig economy has also raised concerns about the long-term sustainability of traditional employment sectors. As more individuals choose freelance and platform-based work over traditional jobs, industries that rely on stable, long-term employment may face challenges in attracting and retaining talent. This could lead to further erosion of traditional employment structures and the need for new approaches to workforce management and economic policy.

Broader Cultural Implications and Debates

Normalization of Digital Content Monetization:

OnlyFans has contributed to the normalization of digital content monetization, particularly in the context of personal and explicit material. The platform has blurred the lines between personal expression and commercial enterprise, leading to debates about the ethics and societal impact of monetizing intimate aspects of one's life. For many creators, OnlyFans represents an opportunity to take control of their financial future and express themselves freely. However, for others, the platform raises concerns about privacy, exploitation, and the commodification of personal identity.

The widespread adoption of OnlyFans and similar platforms has sparked broader cultural debates about the nature of work, privacy, and the value of digital content. These debates often center around the tension between empowerment and exploitation, with some viewing OnlyFans as a platform that empowers individuals to earn a living on their terms, while others see it as a system that encourages the commodification of personal and often explicit material for financial gain.

Impact on Gender Dynamics and Feminism:

OnlyFans has had a significant impact on gender dynamics and the discourse around feminism. The platform is predominantly used by women, who make up the majority of its top earners. For many, OnlyFans has provided a way to achieve financial independence and take control of their bodies and content. This has led to discussions about the role of sex work in feminist discourse, with some arguing that OnlyFans represents a form of empowerment and agency for women in a male-dominated society.

However, this perspective is not without controversy. Critics argue that OnlyFans perpetuates harmful gender stereotypes and reinforces the commodification of women's bodies. They contend that the platform's success is built on the objectification of women, and that it may contribute to the normalization of explicit content in a way that undermines broader efforts to achieve gender equality. These debates reflect the complex and often contradictory nature of the platform's impact on gender dynamics and feminist thought.

Influence on Sexuality and Relationships:

The rise of OnlyFans has also influenced societal views on sexuality and relationships. The platform's focus on personalized and often explicit content has led to a re-examination of traditional notions of intimacy, privacy, and sexual expression. For some, OnlyFans has provided a space for exploring and expressing their sexuality in a safe and controlled environment. This has been particularly important for LGBTQ+ individuals, who may find traditional platforms less welcoming or inclusive.

However, the platform's impact on relationships and sexuality is complex. The commodification of intimacy on OnlyFans has led to concerns about the impact on real-world relationships and the potential for addiction or unhealthy behavior. The platform's focus on monetizing sexual content has also sparked debates about the boundaries between public and private life, and the extent to which individuals should share intimate aspects of their lives online.

Cultural Shifts and the Future of Work:

The success of OnlyFans has contributed to broader cultural shifts in how work is perceived and valued. The platform has challenged traditional notions of what constitutes "real work" and has highlighted the growing importance of digital labor in the modern economy. This shift has been particularly pronounced among younger generations, who are increasingly embracing digital entrepreneurship and rejecting traditional career paths.

OnlyFans has also raised important questions about the future of work in a digital economy. As more individuals turn to platforms like OnlyFans for income, there are concerns about the long-term sustainability of such models, particularly in terms of income security, worker rights, and the potential for exploitation. The platform's success has prompted discussions about the need for new policies and regulations to protect digital workers and ensure that the benefits of the gig economy are equitably distributed.

Ethical and Moral Considerations:

The rise of OnlyFans has also sparked ethical and moral debates about the implications of monetizing personal content, particularly explicit material. These debates often center around the tension between individual autonomy and societal norms, with some arguing that OnlyFans represents a form of empowerment and self-expression, while others see it as contributing to the commodification of personal identity and the erosion of traditional values.

Critics of the platform argue that OnlyFans encourages the exploitation of vulnerable individuals, particularly young people who may be drawn to the platform by the promise of easy money. They contend that the platform's focus on explicit content can lead to unhealthy behavior, addiction, and the objectification of individuals, particularly women. Supporters, on the other hand, argue that OnlyFans provides a safe and controlled environment for individuals to express themselves and earn a living, and that it represents a positive shift towards greater autonomy and control over one's work and identity.

Conclusion: Navigating the Complex Legacy of OnlyFans:

The societal and economic impact of OnlyFans is complex and multifaceted, reflecting broader shifts in the digital economy, employment paradigms, and cultural norms. The platform has empowered many individuals to take control of their financial future and express themselves creatively, but it has also raised important questions about the ethics of content monetization, the risks of the gig economy, and the impact on societal values.

As OnlyFans continues to grow and evolve, it will be important to continue examining its impact on both individuals and society as a whole. The platform's success has highlighted the potential for digital entrepreneurship, but it has also underscored the need for thoughtful regulation and support to ensure that the benefits of the gig economy are equitably distributed and that the risks are adequately managed. The legacy of OnlyFans will likely be one of both empowerment and controversy, reflecting the broader challenges and opportunities of the digital age.

2. Financial Incentives and Content Degradation

How Monetization Influences Content Quality

Revenue Models on OnlyFans: Subscriptions, Pay-Per-View, Tips

Subscriptions:

The primary revenue model on OnlyFans is the subscription-based service, where content creators charge a monthly fee for access to their content. This fee can vary widely depending on the creator's niche, content quality, and audience demand. Subscription prices typically range from as low as $4.99 to upwards of $49.99 per month, although some high-profile creators may charge even more. Creators have the flexibility to set their subscription rates based on their perceived value and audience engagement, allowing them to create a steady stream of income.

The subscription model incentivizes creators to produce regular, high-quality content to retain their subscribers and minimize churn (the rate at which subscribers cancel their subscriptions). Regular content updates, exclusive materials, and engagement with subscribers are crucial to maintaining a loyal subscriber base. This model can lead to a consistent revenue stream, but it also places pressure on creators to continually produce content that meets or exceeds their subscribers' expectations.

Pay-Per-View (PPV) Content:

In addition to the monthly subscription, creators on OnlyFans can offer Pay-Per-View (PPV) content, which allows them to charge subscribers extra for specific pieces of content, such as exclusive videos, photos, or personalized messages. PPV content is often used for premium content that is considered more valuable or tailored to individual subscriber requests. This model enables creators to monetize their most premium content further, offering an additional revenue stream beyond the standard subscription.

The PPV model encourages creators to produce content that is perceived as highly valuable or exclusive, often leading to more explicit or personalized material that can command higher prices. For example, a creator might offer a personalized video message or an exclusive behind-the-scenes video at a higher price point. This model capitalizes on the willingness of subscribers to pay extra for content that feels unique or specially crafted for them.

Tips:

Tipping is another significant revenue stream on OnlyFans. Subscribers can tip creators directly for content they enjoy or during live interactions. Tips can be given as a gesture of appreciation or as a way to request specific content. Tipping is especially popular during live streams, where subscribers can tip in real-time to show support or make requests. The ability to receive tips adds a layer of interactivity and personalization, enhancing the connection between creators and their subscribers.

Tips are often seen as a measure of a creator's success and popularity, with higher tips indicating a more engaged and appreciative audience. Creators who cultivate strong relationships with their subscribers and engage regularly are likely to receive more tips, further boosting their income. However, this also places additional pressure on creators to maintain high levels of interaction and responsiveness, which can be time-consuming and demanding.

Relationship Between Income Potential and Content Choices

Content Quality vs. Quantity:

The revenue models on OnlyFans create a direct relationship between income potential and content choices. Creators who produce high-quality, engaging content are more likely to attract and retain subscribers, leading to a steady stream of income. However, the pressure to produce content consistently can lead some creators to prioritize quantity over quality. The need to maintain a regular posting schedule to keep subscribers engaged may result in content that is rushed or less creative, leading to a potential degradation in overall content quality.

For some creators, the drive to increase income can lead to more explicit or provocative content, especially in niches where such content is in high demand. The competitive nature of OnlyFans, where creators vie for attention in a crowded marketplace, can incentivize creators to push boundaries and produce content that stands out, even if it compromises artistic or personal standards. This phenomenon is particularly evident in the adult content space, where explicit material often commands higher prices and attracts more subscribers.

Niche Specialization:

Creators often find that focusing on a specific niche can lead to higher income potential. Niche specialization allows creators to build a loyal, targeted audience that is willing to pay for content tailored to their interests. However, this focus on niche content can also limit a creator's ability to diversify their offerings, potentially leading to content stagnation. While specialization can be lucrative, it can also trap creators in a cycle of producing similar content to meet subscriber expectations, reducing opportunities for creative experimentation or growth.

For example, a creator who specializes in fitness content might attract subscribers interested in workout videos and diet plans. To maintain this audience, the creator may feel compelled to produce a constant stream of fitness-related content, potentially at the expense of exploring other interests or diversifying their content portfolio. While this can lead to financial success, it can also contribute to content fatigue, both for the creator and their audience.

Personalization and Custom Content:

The income potential on OnlyFans is also closely tied to the level of personalization and custom content a creator is willing to offer. Personalized content, such as custom video messages or private interactions, can command higher prices and increase subscriber loyalty. However, the demand for personalized content can place additional pressure on creators, requiring them to invest more time and effort into producing bespoke material for individual subscribers.

While personalized content can be highly lucrative, it can also be draining for creators who must balance the demands of their general audience with the needs of individual subscribers. The pressure to deliver personalized content can lead to burnout, particularly for creators who rely heavily on this revenue stream. Additionally, the focus on personalization can detract from the overall quality of the content, as creators may prioritize the needs of paying customers over broader creative endeavors.

Impact of Financial Pressures on Creative Decisions

Content Strategy and Financial Incentives:

The financial incentives on OnlyFans have a profound impact on creators' content strategies. Creators who rely on the platform as their primary source of income may feel pressured to produce content that is guaranteed to generate revenue, even if it deviates from their original artistic vision or personal values. This can lead to a shift in content focus, where creators prioritize content that is more likely to attract subscribers and generate tips, often at the expense of creativity and innovation.

For example, a creator who initially joined OnlyFans to share artistic photography may find themselves producing more explicit content if it proves to be more lucrative. The need to meet financial goals can drive creators to make creative compromises, resulting in content that is more commercially driven and less aligned with their original intentions.

Burnout and Content Fatigue:

The pressure to maintain a steady income on OnlyFans can also lead to burnout and content fatigue. Creators who feel compelled to constantly produce new content to satisfy subscriber demand may experience physical and emotional exhaustion. This burnout can manifest in a decline in content quality, as creators may lack the energy or motivation to maintain the same level of creativity and engagement.

Burnout is particularly common among creators who rely heavily on OnlyFans for their livelihood, as the platform's revenue model rewards consistency and regular updates. Creators who are unable to take breaks or reduce their output without risking a loss of income may find themselves trapped in a cycle of overwork and diminishing returns. This can lead to a gradual degradation of content quality as creators struggle to meet the demands of their audience while managing their own well-being.

Ethical Dilemmas and Content Integrity:

The financial pressures on OnlyFans can also create ethical dilemmas for creators. The need to maximize income may lead some creators to produce content that they are uncomfortable with or that compromises their personal values. This is particularly relevant in the adult content space, where creators may feel pressured to produce more explicit material to compete with others or to meet subscriber expectations.

Creators may also face ethical challenges related to the commodification of their personal lives. The platform's focus on personalized and intimate content can blur the lines between public and private life, leading to difficult decisions about how much of themselves they are willing to share for financial gain. These ethical dilemmas can impact content integrity, as creators may feel forced to make choices that align with financial incentives rather than their own values or artistic vision.

Market Saturation and Content Differentiation:

As OnlyFans has grown in popularity, the platform has become increasingly saturated with creators, leading to greater competition for subscribers and tips. This market saturation can make it challenging for new or less-established creators to gain visibility and attract a loyal audience. In response, some creators may feel compelled to produce more extreme or sensational content to stand out in a crowded marketplace.

The pressure to differentiate oneself in a saturated market can lead to a race to the bottom, where creators push the boundaries of content quality and ethics in pursuit of financial success. This dynamic can result in a gradual erosion of content standards, as creators prioritize shock value or explicitness over originality and creativity. The long-term impact of this trend is a potential decline in the overall quality of content on the platform, as creators focus on what sells rather than what inspires.

Conclusion: Balancing Financial Success with Content Quality:

The financial incentives on OnlyFans play a crucial role in shaping content quality and creative decisions. While the platform offers significant opportunities for creators to monetize their content and achieve financial independence, it also presents challenges related to content degradation, burnout, and ethical dilemmas. Creators must navigate these challenges carefully to maintain a balance between financial success and content integrity.

To sustain long-term success on OnlyFans, creators may need to develop strategies that prioritize both quality and consistency, while also managing the pressures of monetization. This may involve setting clear boundaries around content production, diversifying revenue streams, and maintaining a strong connection with their audience without compromising their creative vision or personal values. Ultimately, the ability to balance financial incentives with content quality will be key to sustaining both individual success and the overall health of the platform.

Analysis of Income Streams for Creators on OnlyFans

Breakdown of Typical Earnings for Different Types of Content

1. Subscription-Based Earnings

Low to Mid-Tier Creators:

Creators in the early stages of their OnlyFans journey typically charge between $4.99 to $9.99 per month for subscriptions. These creators often have a smaller, more niche following, with subscriber counts ranging from 100 to 1,000. Their content might include regular updates, behind-the-scenes photos, and videos, as well as personalized shoutouts or interactions to build loyalty among their audience.

- **Example Earnings:** A creator with 300 subscribers paying $7.99 per month would generate approximately $2,397 in subscription revenue before OnlyFans takes its 20% commission. After the commission, the creator would take home around $1,917. As they grow their subscriber base by improving content quality, engagement, and marketing efforts, their earnings could gradually increase.

Mid-Tier to High-Tier Creators:

These creators generally charge between $10.99 to $19.99 per month and have built a substantial following, often ranging from 1,000 to 10,000 subscribers. They typically offer a more polished content strategy, which may include exclusive videos, higher production quality, and regular interaction with their audience through direct messaging or live streams.

- **Example Earnings:** A creator with 5,000 subscribers at $14.99 per month would earn $74,950 before the platform's commission. After OnlyFans takes its 20% cut, the creator would net around $59,960. This income is often supplemented by additional revenue streams, such as PPV content or tips, making this a highly lucrative tier for creators who have managed to cultivate a dedicated fan base.

Top-Tier Creators:

Top-tier creators, often celebrities or well-known influencers, can charge between $20.99 to $49.99 per month, sometimes even more for highly exclusive content. These creators have large followings, often in the tens or hundreds of thousands. Their content might include not only high-quality videos and photos but also personalized and interactive experiences, such as custom content or regular live streams that justify the higher subscription price.

- **Example Earnings:** A top-tier creator with 20,000 subscribers paying $29.99 per month would generate approximately $599,800 in subscription revenue. After the platform's 20% commission, the creator would net around $479,840. The substantial income at this level often allows for further investments in content quality, marketing, and brand collaborations, which can perpetuate growth and engagement.

2. Pay-Per-View (PPV) Content Earnings
General Overview:

PPV content on OnlyFans allows creators to charge an additional fee for access to specific content, such as custom videos, private messages, or exclusive photos. This content is often more personalized or explicit than what is available through standard subscriptions, making it a premium offering. Prices for PPV content can range from $5 to over $100, depending on the exclusivity and customization of the content.

Low to Mid-Tier Creators:

For creators with smaller followings, PPV content can significantly enhance overall earnings. These creators might not have the subscriber numbers to generate large amounts from subscriptions alone, so they leverage PPV content to boost their income. For example, a creator who charges $15 for a custom video and sells it to 50 subscribers could earn an additional $750. If they consistently produce PPV content and market it effectively, they can add several hundred to a few thousand dollars to their monthly earnings.

- **Example Earnings:** A creator with 300 subscribers might sell a $10 custom video to 100 subscribers, earning $1,000 from that single piece of content. Over a month, if they produce and sell multiple PPV items, they could potentially add $2,000 to $5,000 to their monthly income, depending on the frequency and quality of the content.

High-Tier Creators:

High-tier creators can charge premium prices for PPV content, often in the $50 to $200 range, particularly if the content is highly personalized or exclusive. For example, a custom video tailored to a specific request or a one-on-one live session could command a high price. Given their larger following, these creators can sell PPV content to hundreds or even thousands of subscribers, resulting in significant additional revenue.

- **Example Earnings:** A creator with 10,000 subscribers who sells a $100 custom video to 500 of them could generate $50,000 from that single piece of content. If they offer multiple PPV items each month, the additional income can easily exceed $100,000 monthly, making PPV content a critical revenue stream for top-tier creators.

3. Tipping

General Overview:

Tipping allows subscribers to give creators additional money as a gesture of appreciation or in exchange for specific content or actions. Tipping is especially prevalent during live streams, where fans can tip in real-time, but it is also common in direct messages or on content posts. The size of tips can vary widely, from a few dollars to several hundred, depending on the creator's relationship with their subscribers and the value they provide.

Low to Mid-Tier Creators:

For creators with smaller followings, tipping can provide a meaningful boost to their income. These creators might engage more directly with their subscribers, encouraging tips through personalized interactions, shoutouts, or content requests. Tips could range from $5 to $50 per interaction, with overall monthly tips adding up to $200 to $1,000, depending on the level of engagement and the loyalty of their subscriber base.

- **Example Earnings:** A creator who actively encourages tipping through personalized interactions might receive 50 tips of $20 each over the course of a month, adding $1,000 to their income. This can be a significant supplement to their subscription earnings, especially for those who engage regularly and build strong relationships with their subscribers.

High-Tier Creators:

For top-tier creators, tipping can become a substantial part of their income, particularly if they engage in live streaming or offer personalized content frequently. With a large and loyal fan base, these creators might receive tips ranging from $100 to $1,000 or more per session. High-tier creators who regularly engage with their audience can see tips totaling $5,000 to $20,000 or more each month.

- **Example Earnings:** A top-tier creator might receive 200 tips of $50 each during a particularly popular live stream, resulting in $10,000 in tip revenue. If they stream multiple times per week, monthly tipping income could easily exceed $30,000, making it a key component of their overall earnings strategy.

4. Custom Content and Direct Messaging
General Overview:

Custom content and direct messaging offer highly personalized experiences that can command premium prices. Creators can charge for custom videos, photos, or private messages tailored to individual subscriber requests. Direct messaging can also be monetized by charging a fee for one-on-one interactions or personalized responses, allowing creators to build deeper connections with their most dedicated fans.

Low to Mid-Tier Creators:

For creators with a smaller but engaged following, custom content can be a valuable income stream. These creators often charge $20 to $50 for custom videos or photos and might offer additional services such as personalized voice notes or shoutouts. Direct messaging can also be monetized, with creators charging $5 to $20 per message or interaction.

- **Example Earnings:** A creator who offers custom videos at $50 each and sells 20 per month would earn $1,000 from this service. If they also charge for direct messages, bringing in an additional $500 to $1,000 per month, their total earnings from custom content and messaging could range from $1,500 to $2,500.

High-Tier Creators:

High-tier creators can command much higher prices for custom content, often charging $100 to $500 or more for personalized videos or interactions. Given their larger following, they might receive numerous requests for custom content each month, significantly boosting their income. Direct messaging can also be a lucrative revenue stream, with top-tier creators charging $50 to $100 per interaction, depending on the level of personalization and engagement.

- **Example Earnings:** A high-tier creator might sell 50 custom videos at $200 each, generating $10,000 from this service alone. If they also engage in monetized direct messaging, adding another $5,000 to $10,000 per month, their total income from custom content and messaging could easily exceed $20,000 monthly.

Case Studies of Various Income Levels

1. New Creator (0-3 Months):
  Profile:
A new creator, aged 25, focusing on lifestyle and fitness content. This creator has a moderate social media presence, with about 5,000 followers on Instagram and Twitter. They decided to join OnlyFans to monetize their content more directly and build a closer relationship with their audience.
  Subscription Fee:
The creator sets their subscription fee at $9.99 per month, offering a mix of workout routines, diet tips, and behind-the-scenes lifestyle content.
  Earnings:
In the first month, the creator attracts 100 subscribers, generating $999 in subscription revenue. After the platform's 20% commission, they take home approximately $799. They also experiment with a few

PPV items, selling a custom workout video for $10 each to 50 subscribers, earning an additional $500. Tipping and direct messaging bring in another $100. Their total earnings for the first month are around $1,399.

Over the next two months, the creator increases their content output and engagement, growing their subscriber base to 300. With more experience, they offer more PPV content and start charging for personalized diet plans, increasing their total monthly earnings to approximately $3,500 to $4,000.

2. Mid-Tier Creator (6-12 Months):

Profile:

A creator in the cosplay niche, known for their high-quality costumes and detailed tutorials. They have a strong online presence with 50,000 followers across multiple social media platforms, including Instagram, Twitter, and TikTok.

Subscription Fee:

The creator sets their subscription fee at $14.99 per month, offering exclusive cosplay tutorials, progress photos, and live Q&A sessions.

Earnings:

With 1,500 subscribers, the creator earns approximately $22,485 from subscriptions before the platform's commission. After the 20% cut, they take home around $17,988. Additionally, they offer PPV content, such as detailed costume breakdowns and behind-the-scenes videos, priced at $20 each. Selling to 500 subscribers, they earn an additional $10,000 from PPV content.

The creator also engages regularly with their audience through direct messaging, charging $10 per message. With 300 interactions per month, this brings in another $3,000. Tipping, particularly during live streams where they showcase new costumes or provide tutorials, adds another $2,500. Their total monthly earnings are around $33,488.

3. Top-Tier Creator (1-2 Years):

Profile:

A celebrity or influencer who has transitioned to OnlyFans after building a massive following on platforms like Instagram and Twitter, where they have over 1 million followers. They joined OnlyFans to offer exclusive, behind-the-scenes content and engage more personally with their fans.

Subscription Fee:

The creator charges a premium subscription fee of $29.99 per month, offering exclusive content such as personal vlogs, fitness routines, Q&A sessions, and occasional explicit material.

Earnings:

With 50,000 subscribers, this creator generates $1,499,500 from subscriptions alone. After OnlyFans takes its 20% commission, the creator nets around $1,199,600. The creator also frequently offers PPV content, such as custom videos and behind-the-scenes footage, priced at $50 to $100 each. Selling to 10,000 subscribers, they earn an additional $750,000 to $1,000,000 from PPV content monthly.

Tipping is also a significant income source, particularly during live streams where fans can tip to ask questions or request specific actions. Tips can range from $5,000 to $50,000 per month, depending on the level of engagement. Additionally, the creator offers personalized direct messaging, charging $100 per interaction, which could add another $20,000 to $50,000 per month. Their total monthly earnings could easily exceed $2 million.

Role of Supplementary Income Through Sponsorships and Partnerships

1. Sponsorship Deals:

Overview:

As creators grow their following on OnlyFans, they become more attractive to brands looking for sponsorship opportunities. Sponsorship deals typically involve creators promoting a brand's products or services in exchange for payment. These deals can be one-time posts or ongoing partnerships, depending on the brand's marketing strategy and the creator's influence.

Impact on Earnings:

Sponsorship deals can significantly boost a creator's income, particularly for those with a large and engaged audience. A mid-tier creator might earn $2,000 to $5,000 per sponsored post, while top-tier creators could earn $10,000 to $50,000 or more, depending on the brand and the reach of the campaign. These deals are especially lucrative when combined with the creator's subscription, PPV, and tipping income.

Example:

A fitness creator with 100,000 followers on social media and 10,000 subscribers on OnlyFans might land a sponsorship deal with a supplement company. For promoting the company's products in a post and live stream, they could earn $5,000 per post. If they do this weekly, their monthly earnings from sponsorships alone could be $20,000.

2. Affiliate Marketing:

Overview:

Many creators on OnlyFans also engage in affiliate marketing, where they promote products or services and earn a commission on sales generated through their unique referral links. This can include anything from fitness supplements to clothing lines or digital products.

Impact on Earnings:

Affiliate marketing can provide a steady stream of supplementary income, especially for creators in niches like fitness, beauty, or lifestyle. A successful affiliate campaign might bring in an additional $1,000 to $10,000 per month, depending on the products promoted and the creator's audience engagement.

Example:

A beauty creator with 5,000 subscribers might promote a skincare line through affiliate marketing. If they earn a 20% commission on sales and manage to drive $50,000 worth of sales in a month, they would earn $10,000 from affiliate marketing. This income stream, combined with their OnlyFans earnings, would significantly boost their total income.

3. Partnerships and Collaborations:

Overview:

Collaborations with other creators or brands can also be a lucrative income stream. These partnerships might involve co-creating content, participating in joint live streams, or launching a shared product line. Partnerships can also expand a creator's audience by exposing them to new followers.

Impact on Earnings:

Collaborations can lead to increased visibility and subscriber growth, which in turn boosts earnings from subscriptions and PPV content. Additionally, revenue from joint ventures, such as a co-branded merchandise line, can add a significant income stream. For example, a creator might earn an additional $5,000 to $20,000 from a successful collaboration, depending on the scope and success of the partnership.

Example:

Two mid-tier fitness creators might collaborate on a joint workout program, selling access to their combined fan bases. If they price the program at $50 and sell it to 1,000 people, each creator could earn $25,000 from the collaboration. This partnership not only boosts income but also helps each creator reach new potential subscribers.

4. Crowdfunding and Donations:

Overview:

Some creators use crowdfunding platforms like Patreon alongside OnlyFans to diversify their income. These platforms allow fans to support creators through monthly donations, often in exchange for exclusive content or perks not available on OnlyFans.

Impact on Earnings:

While crowdfunding is not as common as direct monetization on OnlyFans, it can still provide a valuable income supplement. Creators might earn an additional $500 to $2,000 per month through crowdfunding, depending on their fan base and the perks offered.

Example:

A creator might use Patreon to offer fans early access to content or exclusive behind-the-scenes footage. If they have 200 patrons each donating $10 per month, they would earn an additional $2,000. Combined with their OnlyFans income, this would further enhance their financial stability.

Conclusion: Diversifying Income for Sustainable Success

The income potential on OnlyFans is significant, but it varies widely depending on the creator's niche, audience size, and engagement strategies. While subscriptions form the backbone of earnings, supplementary income streams like PPV content, tips, sponsorships, and collaborations can significantly enhance a creator's financial success. Creators who diversify their income streams and leverage their audience engagement effectively are more likely to achieve long-term financial sustainability and success on the platform. Diversification not only mitigates risks associated with platform dependency but also provides creators with multiple avenues to maximize their earning potential and build a resilient digital brand.

The Role of Subscriber Demand in Content Creation

Examination of Consumer Preferences

Understanding Subscriber Motivations: Subscriber demand on OnlyFans is primarily driven by the desire for exclusive, personalized, and often intimate content that cannot be accessed elsewhere. Unlike traditional social media platforms, where content is generally free and widely accessible, OnlyFans subscribers are willing to pay for content that offers a deeper connection or more exclusive access to creators. This willingness to pay is often rooted in a desire for closer, more personalized interaction with creators, whether through private messaging, custom content, or live interactions.

Personalization and Exclusivity: Subscribers value content that feels tailored to them. This might include personalized shoutouts, custom videos, or direct engagement through messaging. The more a creator can make a subscriber feel special or valued, the more likely that subscriber is to remain loyal and continue paying for content. This creates a strong incentive for creators to understand and cater to the specific preferences of their audience, often gathering information through direct communication or observing engagement patterns on their posts.

Diversity in Content Types: While many OnlyFans users associate the platform with adult content, consumer preferences on the platform are diverse. Subscribers are interested in a wide range of content types, including fitness, cooking, lifestyle advice, and behind-the-scenes glimpses into the lives of their favorite creators. Understanding the specific interests of their subscriber base allows creators to tailor their content strategy accordingly, ensuring they meet the demand for both general and niche content.

Value for Money: Subscribers are conscious of the value they receive for their money. Creators who provide a high volume of content, regular updates, and interactive opportunities are more likely to retain subscribers. Conversely, creators who fail to meet subscriber expectations in terms of content frequency or quality may see higher churn rates. Therefore, understanding the balance between content quality, frequency, and the pricing of subscriptions is crucial for maintaining a stable subscriber base.

Trends in Popular Content Types and Their Evolution

Adult Content Dominance and Its Evolution: Historically, adult content has been a significant driver of subscriber demand on OnlyFans. However, the nature of this content has evolved over time. Initially, simple photos or videos might have sufficed, but as the platform has grown, so too has the demand for more sophisticated, higher-quality content. Subscribers now expect well-produced, high-definition videos, creative concepts, and even narrative-driven content that goes beyond simple imagery.

The Rise of Fitness and Wellness Content: Over the past few years, there has been a notable increase in demand for fitness and wellness content on OnlyFans. This trend reflects a broader societal focus on health and wellness, with subscribers seeking personalized workout plans, dietary advice, and motivational content. Creators who can offer tailored fitness programs or one-on-one coaching sessions have found a strong niche on the platform, often complementing their subscription-based income with custom workout videos or live training sessions.

Lifestyle and Behind-the-Scenes Content: As OnlyFans has grown, so has the demand for lifestyle and behind-the-scenes content. Subscribers are increasingly interested in seeing the day-to-day lives of their favorite creators, whether through vlogs, daily routine videos, or casual, unfiltered content. This type of content offers a more intimate glimpse into the lives of creators, fostering a deeper connection and making subscribers feel more like part of an exclusive community.

Interactive and Live Content: Interactive content, such as live streams and Q&A sessions, has become increasingly popular on OnlyFans. Subscribers value the opportunity to engage directly with creators in real-time, ask questions, and even influence the direction of the content during live sessions. This trend has led to an increase in live content on the platform, with creators using live streams to foster engagement, solicit tips, and create a sense of immediacy and exclusivity.

Niche and Specialized Content: As the platform has matured, there has been a growing demand for niche and specialized content that caters to specific interests or communities. This includes everything from cosplay and gaming content to educational tutorials and artistic endeavors. Creators who can identify and tap into niche markets often find loyal subscriber bases that are willing to pay a premium for content that caters to their unique interests. The evolution of niche content reflects the platform's broadening appeal and the increasing sophistication of its subscriber base.

Feedback Mechanisms and Their Influence on Content Direction

Direct Messaging and Personalized Feedback: One of the most significant feedback mechanisms on OnlyFans is direct messaging between creators and subscribers. This feature allows subscribers to provide real-time feedback, make content requests, and engage in more personal interactions with creators. For creators, this feedback is invaluable as it provides direct insight into what subscribers want and expect. By responding to these messages and fulfilling requests, creators can tailor their content more closely to subscriber preferences, which can lead to increased subscriber retention and higher earnings through tips and custom content.

Engagement Metrics and Analytics: OnlyFans provides creators with various analytics tools that track subscriber engagement with their content. These metrics include data on the number of views, likes, comments, and shares for each post, as well as information on subscriber demographics and behavior patterns. By analyzing these metrics, creators can identify which types of content perform best, what times of day are most effective for posting, and which content generates the most interaction. This data-driven approach allows creators to refine their content strategies over time, ensuring that they continue to meet subscriber demand and optimize their earnings.

Subscriber Surveys and Polls: Some creators use surveys and polls to gather structured feedback from their subscribers. These tools allow creators to ask specific questions about content preferences, future content ideas, and overall satisfaction with the current offerings. Polls can be particularly effective for gauging interest in new content types or for deciding between multiple content ideas. The direct feedback from these surveys helps creators make informed decisions about their content strategy, ensuring that they align with subscriber interests and expectations.

Trend Analysis and Content Adaptation: Creators on OnlyFans often monitor broader trends within the platform and beyond to stay ahead of subscriber demand. This involves keeping an eye on popular content types, emerging niches, and shifts in subscriber behavior. By staying attuned to these trends, creators can adapt their content strategies to capitalize on new opportunities or shift focus to areas with growing interest. For example, a creator who notices a rising trend in mental wellness content might start incorporating mindfulness videos or stress-relief tips into their offerings, attracting new subscribers who are interested in these topics.

Incorporating Feedback into Content Planning: Feedback from subscribers is not only valuable for refining existing content but also for planning future content. Creators who actively solicit feedback and involve their subscribers in the content creation process can foster a sense of community and loyalty. For example, a creator might ask their subscribers to vote on the theme of the next month's content, choose which costumes to wear, or decide on the topics for upcoming live streams. This collaborative approach not only ensures that the content aligns with subscriber preferences but also strengthens the relationship between creators and their audience, leading to higher engagement and retention rates.

Balancing Subscriber Demand with Creative Integrity: While subscriber demand plays a crucial role in content creation on OnlyFans, creators must also balance this demand with their creative integrity and personal boundaries. There can be pressure to cater to every subscriber request, especially if those requests are financially lucrative. However, creators who maintain a clear sense of their content's direction and purpose are more likely to build a sustainable and fulfilling presence on the platform. This involves setting boundaries around what content they are willing to create, while still being responsive to subscriber preferences and feedback.

Conclusion: Navigating Subscriber Demand for Long-Term Success: Subscriber demand is a powerful force shaping content creation on OnlyFans. Understanding consumer preferences, staying attuned to trends, and leveraging feedback mechanisms are all critical components of a successful content strategy. Creators who can effectively navigate these elements, while balancing their own creative goals and personal boundaries, are more likely to achieve long-term success on the platform. By remaining responsive to subscriber needs and continuously evolving their content offerings, creators can build a loyal, engaged audience that supports sustainable growth and financial stability.

3. The Impact of Provocative Content on OnlyFans

The Rise of Explicit Content on OnlyFans

Historical Context and Initial Content Types on the Platform

Origins of OnlyFans: OnlyFans was launched in 2016 by British entrepreneur Tim Stokely with the idea of creating a platform where content creators could monetize their influence by offering exclusive, behind-the-scenes content directly to their fans. The platform was designed to be a subscription-based service, allowing creators to earn revenue without relying on advertising or third-party sponsorships. From the beginning, the platform was intended to cater to a broad spectrum of creators, including fitness experts, musicians, fashion influencers, and other digital creators looking to capitalize on their social media followings.

Initial Adoption and Early Content: In its early stages, OnlyFans attracted a diverse array of creators who used the platform to share non-explicit content. Fitness trainers, for example, offered workout plans, personalized coaching, and diet tips. Musicians provided fans with exclusive access to new songs, behind-the-scenes footage, and intimate Q&A sessions. Models and fashion influencers shared exclusive photoshoots and styling tips that couldn't be found on their public social media profiles. The platform's early content was primarily focused on providing additional value to fans who were willing to pay for a deeper connection with the creators they admired.

Initial Revenue Models: The revenue model for these creators was relatively straightforward: subscribers paid a monthly fee, typically ranging from $5 to $20, to access this exclusive content. Some creators also experimented with tips and paid private messages as additional revenue streams. At this stage, the platform's focus was on empowering creators to monetize their content and maintain creative control, with the subscription model offering a predictable and sustainable income source.

Transition to More Explicit Content and Reasons Behind It

Emergence of Adult Content Creators: As OnlyFans grew, it began to attract a new demographic of creators—those in the adult entertainment industry. The platform's features, including the ability to directly control pricing, manage content distribution, and interact privately with subscribers, made it an appealing alternative to traditional adult content distribution channels, which were often exploitative and offered lower payouts. The privacy and direct payment systems provided by OnlyFans allowed sex workers and adult performers to bypass traditional gatekeepers, retain more of their earnings, and have greater control over their content and personal safety.

Economic Drivers of Explicit Content: The economic potential of explicit content became apparent as early adopters in the adult industry began sharing their success stories. Creators who had previously struggled to make a living through conventional adult sites found that they could earn significantly more by engaging directly with their audience on OnlyFans. Subscription prices for explicit content were often higher than those for non-explicit content, and the ability to sell pay-per-view (PPV) content, offer custom videos, and receive tips further enhanced income potential. As word spread about the lucrative opportunities on OnlyFans, more creators in the adult industry flocked to the platform, which gradually shifted its content focus.

Cultural Shifts and Social Acceptance: This shift towards explicit content on OnlyFans coincided with broader cultural changes regarding the acceptance of sex work and the destigmatization of adult content. Movements advocating for sex worker rights and the recognition of sex work as legitimate labor gained momentum, and OnlyFans became a symbol of empowerment for many in the industry. The platform allowed creators to operate independently, reduce their reliance on third-party agencies or studios, and interact with their audience on their own terms. The mainstream media also began to take notice, with several high-profile news outlets covering the rise of OnlyFans and its impact on the adult industry.

The Role of the COVID-19 Pandemic: The COVID-19 pandemic was a critical turning point for OnlyFans and the proliferation of explicit content on the platform. With millions of people worldwide losing their jobs or experiencing significant income reductions, many turned to OnlyFans as a means of financial survival. The platform saw a surge in new creators, including those who had never previously considered sharing explicit content. The pandemic also led to an increase in consumer demand for online entertainment, including adult content, as people spent more time at home and sought new forms of interaction and escapism. This period of rapid growth further solidified OnlyFans' reputation as a platform synonymous with explicit content.

Current State and Prevalence of Explicit Content

Dominance of Explicit Content: Today, explicit content is not just prevalent on OnlyFans—it is a defining feature of the platform. While OnlyFans hosts a wide variety of creators, including those offering fitness, cooking, music, and lifestyle content, it is the adult content that has become most associated with the platform. This dominance of explicit material has contributed to the platform's rapid growth and financial success, with many creators earning substantial incomes by catering to the demand for personalized, provocative content.

Diversification Within Explicit Content: The range of explicit content on OnlyFans has diversified significantly, reflecting the varied tastes and preferences of the platform's global user base. Content now spans from amateur and professional pornography to fetish content, erotic photography, and sexual health education. This diversification has allowed creators to carve out specialized niches and build dedicated subscriber bases around specific interests. For example, some creators focus on BDSM content, while others might specialize in cosplay combined with adult themes. The ability to cater to niche markets has been a key factor in the success of many creators, as it allows them to attract and retain subscribers who are looking for specific types of content.

Integration of High Production Values: As the platform has matured, so too have the production values of the content. While OnlyFans initially provided a space for more amateur, self-produced content, many creators have invested in higher production quality as their incomes have increased. This includes professional-grade cameras, lighting, editing software, and sometimes even the hiring of production teams. The improvement in production quality reflects the increasingly competitive nature of the platform, where standing out requires not only engaging content but also a polished and professional presentation. High production values have become particularly important for creators aiming to command higher subscription fees and attract a more discerning audience.

Mainstream Acceptance and Celebrity Participation: The mainstreaming of OnlyFans has also contributed to the normalization of explicit content on the platform. Several celebrities and public figures have joined OnlyFans, either to share exclusive content with their fans or to capitalize on the lucrative opportunities offered by the platform. Notable examples include Cardi B, Bella Thorne, and Tyga, whose participation has brought significant media attention to the platform. While some celebrities have used OnlyFans for non-explicit content, others have pushed the boundaries of what is considered acceptable by traditional celebrity standards, further blurring the lines between mainstream entertainment and adult content.

Challenges and Controversies: The prevalence of explicit content on OnlyFans has not been without controversy. The platform has faced criticism from various quarters, including concerns about the commodification of intimacy, the potential exploitation of creators, and the impact of explicit content on young audiences. Critics argue that the platform's success is built on the objectification of bodies and that it perpetuates harmful stereotypes about sex and relationships. Additionally, there have been concerns about the safety and well-being of creators, particularly those who may feel pressured to produce increasingly explicit content to maintain their income in a highly competitive environment.

Regulatory and Financial Pressures: The dominance of explicit content has also brought regulatory and financial challenges. Payment processors and financial institutions have expressed concerns about the legal and reputational risks associated with adult content, leading to pressure on OnlyFans to implement stricter content guidelines. This culminated in the platform's controversial announcement in August 2021 that it would ban sexually explicit content, a decision that was quickly reversed following backlash from creators and users. The incident highlighted the delicate balance OnlyFans must strike between supporting its creators and complying with the demands of financial and regulatory entities. It also underscored the platform's reliance on explicit content as a core component of its business model.

Efforts to Diversify Content: In response to the challenges associated with hosting explicit content, OnlyFans has made efforts to diversify its content offerings and attract creators from other industries. The platform has launched marketing campaigns aimed at musicians, fitness trainers, chefs, and other non-adult creators, highlighting the potential to monetize a wide range of content types. Additionally,

OnlyFans has introduced features designed to support creators in these categories, such as enhanced content management tools and analytics. While these efforts have had some success, explicit content remains the dominant force on the platform, both in terms of revenue generation and public perception.

Conclusion: The Dual Nature of Explicit Content on OnlyFans

Explicit content has been both a boon and a challenge for OnlyFans. On one hand, it has driven the platform's growth, attracted millions of users, and provided creators with unprecedented opportunities for financial independence and creative control. On the other hand, it has shaped the platform's identity in ways that are complex and often controversial. The rise of explicit content on OnlyFans has raised important questions about the ethics of content creation, the role of digital platforms in regulating adult material, and the broader cultural implications of monetizing intimacy.

As OnlyFans continues to evolve, it will need to navigate the competing pressures of supporting its creator base, managing regulatory and financial risks, and expanding its appeal to a broader audience. The platform's future success will likely depend on its ability to balance these demands while maintaining the trust and loyalty of its creators and subscribers. Whether through the continued dominance of explicit content or a more diversified approach, OnlyFans will remain a significant player in the digital content landscape, shaping the way creators and consumers interact in the online world.

Consequences for Creators and Subscribers on OnlyFans

Short-term and Long-term Effects on Creators' Reputations and Careers

Short-term Effects:

Increased Visibility and Income: In the short term, many creators experience a significant boost in visibility and income after joining OnlyFans, especially if they create explicit content. The platform's direct-to-consumer model allows creators to quickly monetize their work, often leading to substantial earnings within a short period. This financial success can provide immediate benefits, such as financial independence, the ability to pursue personal projects, or investment in higher-quality content production.

Reputation Among Peers and Industry: For some creators, joining OnlyFans can enhance their reputation within certain communities, particularly those that value sexual openness and independence. Creators who successfully leverage OnlyFans to build their brand may gain recognition as savvy entrepreneurs who have harnessed the power of digital platforms to achieve financial success. This can lead to new opportunities, such as collaborations, sponsorships, or even media coverage that further boosts their profile.

Stigma and Negative Perceptions: However, the short-term gains are often accompanied by the potential for stigma and negative perceptions, particularly if the creator is involved in explicit content. Society's attitudes toward sex work and adult content can lead to judgment and discrimination, both online and offline. Creators may face backlash from family, friends, or their broader community, especially if their work on OnlyFans becomes publicly known. This stigma can be exacerbated by the platform's association with adult content, even for those creators who produce non-explicit material.

Career Opportunities and Challenges: While some creators are able to parlay their success on OnlyFans into other career opportunities, such as modeling, acting, or entrepreneurship, others may find their career options limited due to their association with the platform. In industries that are more conservative or traditional, involvement with OnlyFans can be a barrier to employment or professional advancement. Creators may struggle to find work in fields that value a clean, professional image, such as corporate roles, education, or healthcare.

Long-term Effects:

Sustaining Income and Relevance: In the long term, maintaining income and relevance on OnlyFans can be challenging. The platform is highly competitive, and creators must continually produce new content to retain subscribers and attract new ones. Over time, this constant demand can lead to burnout, as creators struggle to balance the need for fresh, engaging content with their personal lives and well-being. Additionally, as the market becomes saturated, it may become increasingly difficult for creators to stand out, leading to a decline in income over time.

Reputation and Career Longevity: Creators who build a strong personal brand on OnlyFans may find long-term success, with the potential to transition into other forms of digital entrepreneurship, such as launching their own websites, creating merchandise, or moving into mainstream media. However, the long-term impact on their reputation can be complex. While some may continue to be celebrated for their entrepreneurial spirit, others may face ongoing challenges due to the stigma associated with explicit content. This stigma can persist even after a creator has left the platform, affecting future career opportunities and personal relationships.

Permanence of Online Content: One of the most significant long-term consequences for creators is the permanence of online content. Once explicit content is shared on OnlyFans, it can be difficult, if not impossible, to fully remove it from the internet. Content may be downloaded, shared, or even leaked without the creator's consent, leading to potential reputational damage that can last for years. This permanence can affect a creator's ability to move on from their OnlyFans career and pursue new opportunities, particularly in more traditional or conservative fields.

Psychological and Emotional Impacts on Both Creators and Subscribers

Psychological Impacts on Creators:

Stress and Anxiety: The pressure to consistently produce and monetize content on OnlyFans can lead to significant stress and anxiety for creators. The platform's competitive nature, combined with the need to maintain subscriber numbers and income, can create a high-pressure environment where creators feel constantly on edge. The fear of losing subscribers, income fluctuations, and the demand for increasingly provocative content can exacerbate these feelings, leading to burnout or mental health issues.

Body Image and Self-Esteem: Creators, particularly those involved in explicit content, may also experience challenges related to body image and self-esteem. The emphasis on physical appearance and the constant scrutiny from subscribers can lead to feelings of inadequacy or pressure to conform to certain beauty standards. Some creators may resort to unhealthy practices, such as extreme dieting or cosmetic procedures, to meet these expectations, which can have long-term negative effects on both physical and mental health.

Isolation and Relationship Strain: The nature of OnlyFans work can also lead to feelings of isolation. Creators may find it difficult to discuss their work with family and friends, leading to a sense of alienation. Additionally, the time and energy required to maintain a successful OnlyFans presence can strain personal relationships, particularly if a partner or family members disapprove of the content being produced. This isolation can contribute to a decline in mental well-being and a sense of disconnection from others.

Psychological Impacts on Subscribers:

Addiction and Compulsion: For some subscribers, the personalized and interactive nature of OnlyFans content can lead to compulsive behavior or addiction. The ability to engage directly with creators, combined with the allure of exclusive content, can create a cycle where subscribers continually seek out more interactions, leading to excessive spending and time investment. This behavior can have negative consequences on a subscriber's personal life, finances, and mental health.

Unrealistic Expectations and Relationship Impact: The nature of content on OnlyFans, particularly explicit material, can also shape subscribers' perceptions of relationships and intimacy. Subscribers may develop unrealistic expectations about real-life relationships, influenced by the curated and often idealized interactions they experience on the platform. This can lead to dissatisfaction in their personal lives, as real-life relationships may not measure up to the fantasy provided by OnlyFans. Additionally, heavy involvement in OnlyFans content can strain existing relationships, particularly if a partner is unaware of or uncomfortable with the subscriber's activities on the platform.

Emotional Attachment and Paranoia: Subscribers who engage frequently with a particular creator may develop emotional attachments, often referred to as parasocial relationships. While these relationships are typically one-sided, the illusion of intimacy can lead to genuine emotional investment from the subscriber. If these feelings are not reciprocated, or if the subscriber feels ignored or slighted by the creator, it can lead to feelings of rejection, loneliness, or even paranoia. In extreme cases, this emotional attachment can escalate into obsessive behavior, with potential risks for both the subscriber and the creator.

Legal Implications and Potential Risks

Legal Risks for Creators:

Content Ownership and Copyright Issues: One of the primary legal concerns for creators on OnlyFans is content ownership and copyright. While creators retain ownership of the content they produce, once it is uploaded to the platform, it is vulnerable to unauthorized distribution. Content can be downloaded, shared, or leaked without the creator's consent, leading to potential legal battles over copyright infringement. Creators must be vigilant in monitoring unauthorized use of their content and may need to engage in legal action to protect their intellectual property rights.

Privacy and Data Security: Privacy is another significant concern for creators, particularly those producing explicit content. While OnlyFans provides some level of privacy protection, such as allowing creators to block users from specific regions, there is always the risk of doxxing (the unauthorized release of personal information) or hacking. Creators who are doxxed may face harassment, threats, or even physical danger, making privacy and data security critical issues. Additionally, the platform itself may be vulnerable to data breaches, potentially exposing sensitive information about creators and subscribers.

Legal Compliance and Age Verification: Creators must also navigate the legal requirements for producing and distributing adult content, including ensuring that all participants are of legal age and have provided informed consent. Failure to comply with these regulations can result in serious legal consequences, including criminal charges. OnlyFans requires creators to undergo age verification, but creators are also responsible for ensuring that their content complies with local and international laws regarding pornography and explicit material. Additionally, creators must be aware of the legal implications of producing content that may be accessible to underage viewers or that violates obscenity laws in certain jurisdictions.

Employment and Contractual Risks: Creators who work on OnlyFans while employed in other jobs may face risks related to their employment contracts or workplace policies. Many employers have strict policies regarding conduct outside of work, particularly related to adult content. Creators could face disciplinary action, including termination, if their OnlyFans activity is deemed to violate these policies. Furthermore, creators who have signed non-disclosure agreements (NDAs) or other restrictive covenants in their employment contracts may inadvertently breach these agreements through their OnlyFans activity, leading to potential legal disputes.

Legal Risks for Subscribers:

Unauthorized Distribution and Legal Liability: Subscribers who download and share content from OnlyFans without the creator's consent may face legal action for copyright infringement. While many subscribers may not be aware of the legal implications of redistributing content, doing so can result in significant legal consequences, including fines or lawsuits. Additionally, sharing explicit content without consent can lead to criminal charges in some jurisdictions, particularly if the content is shared with the intent to harm or harass the creator.

Privacy and Data Security for Subscribers: Subscribers also face privacy and data security risks when using OnlyFans. The platform requires users to provide payment information, which could be vulnerable to hacking or data breaches. If a subscriber's involvement with OnlyFans becomes public, particularly if they have been purchasing explicit content, they may face personal or professional repercussions, including damage to their reputation or relationships. Subscribers must be cautious about the personal information they share on the platform and consider using secure payment methods to protect their privacy.

Potential Legal Implications of Interaction: Subscribers who engage in inappropriate or illegal interactions with creators may face legal consequences. For example, attempting to coerce a creator into producing illegal content, such as material involving minors or non-consensual acts, can result in criminal charges. Additionally, subscribers who engage in harassment, stalking, or other forms of online abuse may be subject to legal action, including restraining orders or criminal prosecution.

Conclusion: Navigating the Complexities of OnlyFans

The consequences of participating in OnlyFans, both as a creator and as a subscriber, are multifaceted and extend beyond the immediate financial rewards or entertainment value. Creators must navigate a landscape fraught with potential reputational, psychological, and legal challenges, while subscribers also face risks related to privacy, emotional health, and legal liability. As the platform continues to evolve, it is essential for both creators and subscribers to be aware of these risks and take proactive steps to mitigate them.

For creators, this might involve setting clear boundaries around their content, investing in legal and financial advice, and ensuring they are prepared for the long-term implications of their work on the platform. For subscribers, it means being mindful of their interactions, protecting their privacy, and understanding the legal responsibilities associated with consuming and sharing content. Ultimately, the success of OnlyFans as a platform will depend on how well it can support and protect its users while navigating the complex social, legal, and ethical landscape in which it operates.

Societal Perceptions and Backlash Against OnlyFans

Public Opinion and Media Portrayal of OnlyFans

Initial Media Coverage and Growing Popularity: When OnlyFans first gained widespread attention, the media coverage was largely focused on the platform's innovative approach to content monetization and the opportunities it provided for creators to earn substantial income. Stories about successful creators who made significant amounts of money in a short period were common, with headlines often highlighting the platform as a game-changer for digital entrepreneurs. This initial coverage was generally positive, emphasizing the empowerment of creators who were able to take control of their content and finances.

Shift in Narrative with the Rise of Explicit Content: As the platform became more associated with explicit content, the media narrative began to shift. OnlyFans started to be portrayed as a hub for adult entertainment, and the conversation around it became more complex. While some media outlets continued to highlight the financial success of creators, others began to focus on the ethical and societal implications of the platform. Headlines began to reflect concerns about the commodification of intimacy, the potential exploitation of young creators, and the blurring of lines between mainstream social media and adult content.

Mainstream Media and Celebrity Involvement: The involvement of celebrities and influencers on OnlyFans brought the platform even further into the mainstream media spotlight. Celebrities like Cardi B, Bella Thorne, and Tyga joined the platform, generating significant media attention and bringing new users to the site. However, this also sparked controversy, particularly when celebrities were perceived as overshadowing smaller creators or when their involvement led to platform changes that negatively affected other users. For example, Bella Thorne's presence on OnlyFans in 2020 led to widespread criticism after she reportedly earned $1 million in 24 hours, resulting in platform policy changes that impacted all creators, particularly those relying on smaller, more frequent transactions.

Public Opinion: Public opinion on OnlyFans is deeply divided. For some, the platform is seen as a symbol of empowerment, providing individuals with the means to control their content and earn a living on their own terms. Supporters argue that OnlyFans has democratized content creation, allowing creators to bypass traditional gatekeepers and connect directly with their audience. On the other hand, there is significant criticism of the platform, particularly from more conservative segments of society. Critics argue that OnlyFans promotes the commodification of intimacy and contributes to the normalization of pornography, which they believe has negative societal implications, especially for younger generations.

Media Backlash and Controversies: OnlyFans has also been the subject of numerous media controversies, often focusing on issues such as the platform's role in sex work, the potential exploitation of young and vulnerable individuals, and concerns about content leaks and privacy breaches. These controversies have fueled public debates about the platform's ethical implications, with some media outlets taking a sensationalist approach, framing OnlyFans as a dangerous or morally corrupting force. This negative portrayal has contributed to the stigma surrounding the platform and its users, even as it continues to grow in popularity.

Analysis of Moral and Ethical Criticisms

Commodification of Intimacy: One of the most significant ethical criticisms of OnlyFans is that it commodifies intimacy and personal relationships. Critics argue that the platform encourages individuals to monetize aspects of their personal lives that would traditionally be private, such as sexual experiences or intimate interactions. This commodification is seen as problematic because it reduces complex human experiences to transactions, potentially leading to a devaluation of intimacy and a distorted understanding of relationships, particularly for younger audiences who may be influenced by the content they see on the platform.

Exploitation and Vulnerability: Another major ethical concern is the potential for exploitation on OnlyFans. Critics argue that the platform's financial incentives may push vulnerable individuals, particularly young people, into producing explicit content that they might not otherwise create. The allure of quick money can lead some creators to compromise their values or engage in risky behavior, with long-term consequences that they may not fully understand. There are also concerns about the power dynamics between creators and subscribers, with the potential for coercion or manipulation in exchange for financial gain.

Impact on Society and Culture: The broader societal impact of OnlyFans is also a point of contention. Some critics believe that the platform contributes to the normalization of pornography and the erosion of traditional values related to sex and relationships. They argue that the widespread availability and consumption of explicit content can have negative effects on individuals and society as a whole, including desensitization to sexual content, increased objectification of bodies, and a shift in cultural attitudes towards sex and intimacy. These critics often express concern about the platform's influence on younger generations, who may be exposed to adult content at an impressionable age.

Privacy and Consent Issues: Privacy and consent are also central to the ethical debates surrounding OnlyFans. While the platform offers creators control over their content, there are still significant risks related to privacy and the unauthorized distribution of material. Content leaks, where private or paid-for content is shared without the creator's consent, are a common issue on the platform. These leaks can have devastating effects on creators, particularly if explicit content is made public without their permission. Additionally, the platform's global reach means that creators must navigate varying legal standards and cultural attitudes towards explicit content, which can complicate issues of consent and privacy.

Long-term Consequences for Creators: Critics also highlight the potential long-term consequences for creators who share explicit content on OnlyFans. The permanence of online content means that material shared today could resurface in the future, potentially impacting a creator's personal life, career prospects, or mental health. The stigma associated with sex work and adult content can lead to discrimination or social ostracization, even after a creator has left the platform. These long-term risks raise ethical questions about the responsibilities of the platform and society in supporting individuals who choose to participate in OnlyFans.

Responses from Creators and the Platform to Societal Backlash

Creators' Responses:

Empowerment and Agency: Many creators respond to societal backlash by framing their participation on OnlyFans as an act of empowerment and agency. They argue that the platform allows them to take control of their bodies, their content, and their financial futures in ways that were not previously possible. For these creators, OnlyFans is a means of breaking free from traditional employment structures, which may be exploitative or limiting, and instead building a career on their own terms. They also emphasize the autonomy they have in deciding what content to produce and how to interact with their audience, challenging the notion that they are being exploited or coerced.

Destigmatization of Sex Work: A significant number of creators also use their platform to advocate for the destigmatization of sex work. They argue that sex work is legitimate work and should be treated as such, with the same rights and protections afforded to other forms of labor. These creators often engage in activism, educating their audience about the realities of sex work and pushing back against the stereotypes and prejudices that contribute to the stigma surrounding their profession. By sharing their experiences and building supportive communities, they seek to change public perceptions and create a more accepting environment for sex workers.

Reframing the Narrative: Some creators actively work to reframe the narrative around their participation on OnlyFans. Rather than focusing solely on the financial aspects, they highlight the creative and artistic elements of their work. For example, photographers, models, and performers might emphasize the craftsmanship that goes into producing high-quality content, whether it's through innovative photoshoots, carefully curated aesthetics, or the storytelling elements of their videos. By presenting their work as a form of art or performance, these creators challenge the simplistic view that OnlyFans is solely about explicit content and monetary gain.

Transparency and Education: To address concerns about exploitation and vulnerability, some creators take a proactive approach by being transparent about their experiences on the platform and educating their audience about the realities of working on OnlyFans. They share insights into the challenges and risks involved, such as managing privacy, dealing with stigma, and navigating the complexities of content creation. By providing this information, they aim to empower others to make informed decisions about whether to join the platform and how to protect themselves if they do. This transparency also helps to build trust with their audience, reinforcing the idea that creators are in control of their own narratives.

Platform's Responses:

Policy Adjustments and Creator Protections: In response to societal backlash and the concerns raised by both creators and the public, OnlyFans has made several policy adjustments aimed at protecting creators and ensuring the platform's sustainability. For example, OnlyFans has introduced stricter verification processes to prevent underage users from accessing the platform and to ensure that all content is produced and shared consensually. The platform has also implemented measures to combat content piracy and unauthorized distribution, such as watermarking content and providing tools for creators to take down stolen material from other websites.

Efforts to Diversify Content: OnlyFans has also made efforts to diversify the types of content available on the platform in response to criticisms that it is overly reliant on explicit material. The platform has launched campaigns to attract creators from a wide range of industries, including fitness, cooking, music, and education. By promoting the platform as a space for all types of creators, OnlyFans aims to shift the public perception away from its association with adult content and present itself as a more inclusive and multifaceted platform. However, the effectiveness of these efforts is still debated, as explicit content continues to dominate the platform's revenue and public image.

Addressing Legal and Ethical Concerns: OnlyFans has taken steps to address the legal and ethical concerns raised by critics, particularly around issues of consent and exploitation. The platform has worked to enhance its content moderation practices, ensuring that creators are aware of and comply with relevant laws and regulations. OnlyFans has also increased its efforts to provide resources and support for creators, including mental health resources and guidance on how to manage their online presence safely. These initiatives are part of a broader strategy to demonstrate the platform's commitment to responsible content creation and to mitigate the risks associated with its use.

Public Relations and Brand Management: To manage its public image, OnlyFans has invested in public relations campaigns aimed at highlighting the positive aspects of the platform. These campaigns often focus on the success stories of creators who have used OnlyFans to achieve financial independence, build their personal brands, or fund creative projects. The platform also emphasizes its role in supporting small creators and providing a space for diverse voices that might not have a platform elsewhere. By promoting these narratives, OnlyFans seeks to counterbalance the negative media coverage and public criticism it has received.

Conclusion: Navigating Societal Perceptions and Backlash

The societal perceptions and backlash against OnlyFans reflect broader tensions around issues of sex work, digital privacy, and the commodification of personal content. While the platform has provided unprecedented opportunities for many creators, it has also sparked significant ethical and moral debates. The responses from both creators and the platform itself highlight the complexities of operating in this space, where issues of empowerment, exploitation, and societal norms intersect.

As OnlyFans continues to evolve, it will need to navigate these challenges carefully, balancing the need to protect its creators, address public concerns, and sustain its business model. For creators, the ongoing societal backlash underscores the importance of transparency, education, and community support in navigating the risks and rewards of working on the platform. Ultimately, the future of OnlyFans will depend on its ability to adapt to changing societal attitudes and regulatory landscapes while continuing to provide a viable and empowering platform for its users.

4. Ethical Considerations in the OnlyFans Ecosystem

The Erosion of Traditional Ethical Standards

Comparison of Ethical Norms in Traditional vs. Digital Media

Traditional Media Ethics: In traditional media, ethical standards have been shaped by long-established norms and regulations that prioritize principles like truthfulness, objectivity, respect for privacy, and the protection of vulnerable individuals. Journalists, broadcasters, and content creators in traditional media are often guided by professional codes of conduct that emphasize responsible reporting, the avoidance of sensationalism, and the need to consider the potential impact of their work on audiences. These standards are reinforced by regulatory bodies, such as the Federal Communications Commission (FCC) in the United States, which set and enforce rules to ensure that content adheres to these ethical guidelines.

In the realm of entertainment, similar ethical considerations apply. Film, television, and advertising industries are subject to guidelines that regulate the depiction of sex, violence, and other sensitive topics. These guidelines often require content creators to balance artistic expression with social responsibility, ensuring that their work does not contribute to harm or perpetuate negative stereotypes.

Digital Media and the Shift in Ethical Norms: With the rise of digital media, including platforms like OnlyFans, traditional ethical standards have been challenged by the decentralized and user-generated nature of online content. Unlike traditional media, where content is often subject to editorial oversight and regulatory scrutiny, digital platforms operate with far less oversight. This has led to a more permissive environment where creators have greater freedom to produce and distribute content according to their own standards, often without the same level of accountability.

The lack of centralized regulation in digital media has contributed to a shift in ethical norms. Content that would be considered inappropriate or unethical in traditional media can find a home on platforms like OnlyFans, where creators are empowered to set their own boundaries and cater to niche audiences. This shift has led to the erosion of some traditional ethical standards, as creators and platforms prioritize engagement, profitability, and personal autonomy over the ethical considerations that have historically governed media production.

Factors Contributing to Ethical Compromises

Economic Pressures and Financial Incentives: One of the most significant factors contributing to ethical compromises on OnlyFans is the platform's strong financial incentives. The promise of significant earnings can lead creators to push ethical boundaries in pursuit of higher income. For example, creators might produce increasingly explicit content, despite personal discomfort, because it attracts more subscribers or generates higher tips. The pressure to maintain and grow income can also lead creators to engage in behavior that they might otherwise avoid, such as producing content that objectifies or exploits themselves or others.

Economic pressures are particularly acute for creators who rely on OnlyFans as their primary source of income. The platform's competitive nature means that creators must continually produce new content to retain subscribers, leading to a constant pressure to innovate or escalate the intensity of their material. This environment can foster a mindset where ethical considerations are sidelined in favor of financial success.

The Influence of Audience Demand: Audience demand plays a crucial role in shaping the ethical landscape on OnlyFans. The platform's interactive nature allows subscribers to directly influence the content that creators produce, often through requests, tips, or feedback. While this can lead to personalized and engaging content, it can also result in ethical dilemmas when subscribers push for content that crosses the creator's personal boundaries or societal norms. Creators may feel pressured to meet these demands to maintain their subscriber base, leading to ethical compromises.

Additionally, the anonymity of online interactions can embolden subscribers to make more extreme or inappropriate requests, further complicating the ethical considerations for creators. The desire to please subscribers and maximize earnings can create a situation where creators feel compelled to produce content that they might not be comfortable with, potentially leading to long-term consequences for their mental health and well-being.

The Lack of Oversight and Regulation: The decentralized nature of digital platforms like OnlyFans means that there is little external oversight or regulation of content. While the platform has community guidelines and content moderation practices, these are often less stringent than the regulations governing traditional media. This lack of oversight allows for greater freedom of expression but also opens the door to ethical lapses, as creators operate in an environment with fewer checks and balances.

The absence of strict regulatory frameworks can lead to a culture where the pursuit of profit overrides ethical considerations. For example, creators might engage in misleading marketing practices, such as using clickbait or exaggerating the exclusivity of their content, to attract subscribers. Similarly, the lack of regulation can make it easier for exploitative or harmful content to proliferate, as there are fewer mechanisms in place to prevent or address such issues.

Case Studies Highlighting Ethical Dilemmas Faced by Creators

Case Study 1: The Pressure to Escalate Content

Background: A creator who joined OnlyFans to share fitness and lifestyle content gradually began incorporating more suggestive material after noticing that these posts received higher engagement and tips. Over time, the creator found themselves producing content that was increasingly explicit, despite their initial intentions to keep their material within certain boundaries.

Ethical Dilemma: The creator faced an ethical dilemma as they grappled with the decision to continue escalating their content or return to their original, less explicit focus. On one hand, the explicit content was highly lucrative, leading to a significant increase in income. On the other hand, the creator felt uncomfortable with the direction their content had taken, particularly as it conflicted with their personal values and the image they had initially wanted to project.

Resolution: The creator ultimately decided to scale back the explicit content and refocus on their original niche, despite the potential loss of income. They communicated this decision to their subscribers, emphasizing their commitment to authenticity and personal integrity. While some subscribers left, others appreciated the transparency and stayed on, supporting the creator's decision to prioritize ethical considerations over financial gain.

Case Study 2: Responding to Inappropriate Subscriber Requests

Background: A popular OnlyFans creator regularly received requests from subscribers for custom content. While most requests were within the creator's comfort zone, some subscribers began asking for content that the creator found morally questionable or degrading. These requests were often accompanied by substantial tips, creating a financial incentive to comply.

Ethical Dilemma: The creator was faced with the ethical dilemma of whether to fulfill these requests in exchange for the financial rewards or to reject them in order to maintain their personal ethical standards. The pressure to meet subscriber demands while maintaining a profitable business added complexity to the situation.

Resolution: The creator chose to set clear boundaries with their subscribers, explicitly stating the types of content they were willing to create and refusing requests that crossed those boundaries. They also used the platform's tools to block or mute subscribers who continued to push for inappropriate content. By taking a firm stance, the creator maintained their ethical integrity and continued to build a loyal subscriber base that respected their boundaries.

Case Study 3: The Risks of Content Leaks and Privacy Violations

Background: A creator who produced explicit content on OnlyFans discovered that some of their material had been leaked online without their consent. The leak not only violated the creator's privacy but also led to significant personal and professional challenges, including harassment and damage to their reputation.

Ethical Dilemma: The creator faced the ethical dilemma of whether to continue producing content on OnlyFans, knowing the risks of further privacy violations, or to leave the platform altogether. Additionally, the creator had to consider the ethical implications of how to respond to the leak, whether through legal action or other means.

Resolution: The creator decided to take legal action against the individuals responsible for the leak, working with OnlyFans to remove the unauthorized content from other websites. They also took steps to enhance their privacy and security, such as using pseudonyms, watermarking content, and limiting personal interactions with subscribers. Despite the challenges, the creator chose to remain on

OnlyFans, using their experience to advocate for better protections and support for all creators on the platform.

Conclusion: Navigating Ethical Challenges in the Digital Age

The OnlyFans ecosystem presents unique ethical challenges for creators, driven by the platform's financial incentives, audience demands, and lack of traditional oversight. As creators navigate this landscape, they are often forced to make difficult decisions that balance profitability with personal integrity and societal norms. The case studies highlighted here illustrate the complexities of these ethical dilemmas and the varied ways in which creators respond to them.

Ultimately, the erosion of traditional ethical standards in digital media underscores the need for a more nuanced understanding of the responsibilities and challenges faced by creators in the digital age. As platforms like OnlyFans continue to evolve, it will be important for creators, subscribers, and the broader society to engage in ongoing dialogue about the ethical implications of this new media landscape, and to develop strategies for ensuring that ethical considerations remain at the forefront of content creation.

Challenges Faced by Creators in Maintaining Integrity

Balancing Financial Needs with Personal Values

The Pressure to Monetize: One of the most significant challenges creators face on platforms like OnlyFans is the need to balance their financial goals with their personal values. The platform's structure, which heavily incentivizes content that attracts high engagement and subscriber retention, often places creators in situations where they must decide whether to prioritize income or adhere to their ethical standards. For many creators, especially those who rely on OnlyFans as their primary source of income, this can lead to a difficult tension between producing content that aligns with their values and generating the revenue needed to support themselves and their families.

Examples of Value Conflicts: Creators might struggle with the decision to produce more explicit or provocative content if it is not in line with their personal beliefs or desired public image, but doing so could significantly increase their earnings. This conflict is particularly pronounced in an environment where explicit content tends to draw more subscribers and tips. The pressure to escalate content, either in frequency or in explicitness, can lead creators to cross boundaries they initially set for themselves, resulting in internal conflict and potential long-term regrets.

Coping Strategies: To manage this balance, some creators set clear boundaries from the outset regarding the types of content they are willing to produce. This might involve establishing specific limits on explicitness, the nature of subscriber interactions, or the kinds of requests they are willing to fulfill. Others might diversify their income streams, using OnlyFans as one part of a broader portfolio that includes other forms of content creation or digital work, thereby reducing the pressure to compromise their values for financial gain.

Case Study: A creator who initially joined OnlyFans to share fashion and lifestyle content might find themselves gradually shifting towards more revealing or sexualized content due to subscriber demand and the higher income it generates. Over time, this shift could lead to discomfort as the creator realizes that their current content no longer reflects their original intentions or values. To address this, the creator might decide to scale back the explicitness of their content, communicate this change to their subscribers, and explore additional revenue streams, such as brand partnerships or merchandise, to supplement their income.

Navigating Platform Policies and Community Guidelines

Understanding and Complying with Guidelines: OnlyFans, like other digital platforms, has a set of community guidelines and content policies that creators must adhere to. These guidelines are designed to ensure that content on the platform is safe, legal, and in compliance with international laws and regulations. However, navigating these guidelines can be challenging for creators, particularly when the rules are ambiguous or subject to change. For example, creators might struggle with understanding the specific limits on explicit content, or with complying with policies related to age verification, privacy, and consent.

Impact of Policy Changes: OnlyFans has periodically updated its policies, sometimes in response to external pressures from financial institutions, regulators, or public outcry. These changes can create significant challenges for creators, especially if new rules restrict the types of content they can produce or change the way they interact with subscribers. Creators may feel that their content is being unfairly targeted or that they are being forced to change their business model to remain compliant, which can lead to frustration and a sense of instability.

Case Study: In August 2021, OnlyFans announced a policy change that would ban sexually explicit content, a decision that was quickly reversed after backlash from creators and users. During the brief period of uncertainty, many creators faced significant stress as they contemplated the potential loss of their primary income stream. This incident highlighted the precarious nature of relying on a platform that can change its policies at any time, and underscored the importance of diversifying income sources and staying informed about policy updates.

Managing Compliance and Content Strategy: To navigate these challenges, creators must stay informed about platform policies and be proactive in adjusting their content strategies to ensure compliance. This might involve regularly reviewing the platform's guidelines, participating in creator forums or networks to share information, and seeking legal or professional advice if necessary. Some creators also choose to build a presence on multiple platforms, reducing their dependency on any one site and spreading the risk associated with policy changes.

Case Study: A creator who specializes in fetish content might face challenges if OnlyFans updates its guidelines to restrict certain types of explicit material. To adapt, the creator might start exploring other platforms that are more permissive or begin offering non-explicit content that still appeals to their audience. By diversifying their content and platform presence, the creator can protect their income while continuing to engage with their audience in a way that aligns with their values and the platform's policies.

Peer Pressure and Competition Among Creators

The Competitive Landscape: OnlyFans is a highly competitive platform, with millions of creators vying for subscribers' attention and financial support. This competition can create pressure to produce more content, more frequently, and to push boundaries in ways that might not align with a creator's personal values or comfort levels. The desire to stand out in a crowded marketplace can lead creators to engage in behaviors they might otherwise avoid, such as underpricing their content, engaging in risky interactions with subscribers, or producing content that they feel compromises their integrity.

Impact of Peer Comparisons: Creators on OnlyFans often compare themselves to their peers, particularly those who are highly successful or have large followings. Seeing other creators achieve significant financial success can lead to feelings of inadequacy or pressure to replicate their strategies, even if those strategies involve ethical compromises or personal discomfort. This peer pressure can be particularly challenging for new or less established creators who are still building their audience and might feel compelled to take risks to catch up with more successful peers.

Coping with Competition: To navigate the pressures of competition, some creators focus on building a unique brand or niche that differentiates them from others on the platform. By emphasizing what makes their content or approach special, creators can attract an audience that appreciates their individuality and is less focused on explicitness or quantity. Additionally, some creators form support networks with their peers, offering advice, encouragement, and collaboration opportunities that help them maintain their integrity while growing their audience.

Case Study: A creator who primarily shares artistic nude photography might feel pressured to produce more explicit content after seeing peers who produce similar content but with a more sexualized angle achieve greater financial success. Rather than compromising their artistic vision, the creator might choose to double down on their niche, emphasizing the quality and artistry of their work. They could also seek out collaborations with other creators who share their values, building a supportive community that reinforces their commitment to integrity.

Building a Supportive Community: Creators who successfully navigate these challenges often do so by building a supportive community of peers and subscribers who respect their boundaries and share their values. By cultivating a loyal audience that appreciates their content for its uniqueness and authenticity, creators can reduce the pressure to conform to the more competitive or explicit norms of the platform. Engaging with like-minded creators and participating in ethical discussions within the community can also help creators stay grounded and focused on their long-term goals.

Conclusion: Upholding Integrity in a Challenging Environment

Maintaining integrity on a platform like OnlyFans requires creators to balance multiple challenges, including financial pressures, platform policies, and competition from peers. By setting clear boundaries, staying informed about guidelines, and focusing on their unique strengths, creators can navigate these challenges while staying true to their personal values. Building a supportive community, both among subscribers and fellow creators, is crucial for sustaining this balance and ensuring long-term success on the platform. Ultimately, the ability to maintain integrity in the face of these challenges is key to building a sustainable and fulfilling career in the OnlyFans ecosystem.

The Platform's Policies and Their Effectiveness

Overview of OnlyFans' Terms of Service and Content Guidelines

Terms of Service (ToS): OnlyFans' Terms of Service (ToS) provide the legal framework governing the use of the platform by both creators and subscribers. These terms outline the rights and responsibilities of users, including content ownership, payment processing, privacy, and acceptable use. The ToS specify that creators retain ownership of the content they produce, but by posting on OnlyFans, they grant the platform a license to use, display, and distribute the content within the scope of the service. Additionally, the ToS detail the platform's policies on refunds, account termination, and dispute resolution.

Content Guidelines: OnlyFans' content guidelines define what types of content are permissible on the platform. These guidelines prohibit certain forms of content, such as hate speech, harassment, non-consensual pornography, illegal activities, and the depiction of minors in any sexual context. The platform also has rules against promoting violence, drugs, and weapons. While OnlyFans is known for allowing adult content, it does enforce specific rules regarding explicit material, such as requiring creators to verify their age and the age of any participants in their content.

Age Verification and Consent: A key component of OnlyFans' policies is the requirement for age verification. Creators must provide proof of age (18 or older) before they can start posting content. This verification process also applies to any collaborators who appear in a creator's content. Additionally, OnlyFans requires that all content be consensual, and creators must adhere to legal standards regarding consent and privacy. This includes obtaining explicit consent from any individuals featured in their content and ensuring that no content is uploaded without the consent of all parties involved.

Financial Policies: OnlyFans has established financial policies that govern how creators are paid and how subscribers are charged. Creators can set their own subscription prices and offer additional content through pay-per-view (PPV) or tips. The platform takes a 20% commission on all earnings, with the remaining 80% going to the creator. OnlyFans also has policies in place to handle disputes over payments, such as chargebacks, and to protect against fraudulent activity.

Analysis of Enforcement Mechanisms and Their Consistency

Content Moderation: OnlyFans employs a combination of automated systems and human moderators to enforce its content guidelines. Automated systems are used to detect and flag potentially problematic content, such as illegal material or content that violates the platform's terms. Human moderators then review flagged content to determine whether it should be removed or whether further action is needed, such as account suspension or termination.

Inconsistencies in Enforcement: Despite these mechanisms, there have been reports of inconsistencies in how OnlyFans enforces its policies. Some creators have expressed frustration with the platform's moderation practices, citing cases where content that clearly violated guidelines remained online, while other content was removed without a clear explanation. These inconsistencies can be attributed to several factors, including the sheer volume of content uploaded to the platform daily and the challenges of moderating nuanced or context-specific issues, such as the difference between artistic nudity and explicit content.

Challenges with Automated Moderation: Automated moderation systems, while efficient, are prone to errors, especially in contexts that require understanding of nuance or intent. For example, a system might flag content that includes nudity, even if it is presented in an artistic or non-sexualized manner. Conversely, explicit content might slip through if it doesn't match predefined patterns used by the system. These limitations highlight the importance of human moderators in ensuring that content is evaluated fairly and in context, but they also reveal the challenges of scaling moderation efforts to effectively manage the vast amount of content on the platform.

Handling of Violations and Disputes: When content is found to violate OnlyFans' guidelines, the platform may take several actions, including content removal, issuing warnings to creators, or suspending or terminating accounts. However, creators have reported that the process for appealing these decisions can be opaque and inconsistent. Some creators feel that their appeals are not given proper consideration, or that they receive generic responses that do not address the specifics of their case. This can lead to a lack of trust in the platform's enforcement mechanisms and a sense of insecurity among creators who are unsure whether their content will be deemed acceptable.

Selective Enforcement Concerns: There have also been concerns about selective enforcement, where certain creators or types of content are more heavily scrutinized or penalized than others. This can be particularly problematic in cases where creators feel that they are being targeted for reasons unrelated to the content itself, such as their identity, niche, or the size of their following. Selective enforcement undermines the credibility of the platform's policies and can create an environment where creators feel they are not being treated fairly.

Impact on Creators: Inconsistent or unclear enforcement of policies can have significant consequences for creators. Those who inadvertently violate guidelines may lose income if their content is removed or if their accounts are suspended. Additionally, the fear of enforcement actions can lead to self-censorship, where creators avoid producing certain types of content even if it technically complies with the platform's rules. This can stifle creativity and limit the diversity of content available on OnlyFans.

Recommendations for Policy Improvements

Enhance Transparency and Communication: OnlyFans could improve the transparency of its enforcement processes by providing creators with clearer explanations when content is flagged, removed, or when accounts are penalized. This could include detailed information on why a particular piece of content violated the guidelines, as well as suggestions for how to modify the content to comply with the rules. Improving communication during the appeals process is also crucial, as it would help creators feel that their concerns are being heard and addressed fairly.

Strengthen Human Moderation: While automated systems are necessary for managing the vast amount of content on the platform, OnlyFans should invest in strengthening its human moderation capabilities. This could involve increasing the number of human moderators and providing them with additional training to better understand the context and nuances of different types of content. A stronger human moderation team would help reduce the inconsistencies and errors that arise from relying too heavily on automated systems.

Develop Clearer Guidelines: To reduce confusion and improve compliance, OnlyFans should consider revising its content guidelines to make them more specific and easier to understand. This could include providing more concrete examples of what constitutes a violation and offering more detailed guidance on areas that are often subject to interpretation, such as the line between artistic expression and explicit content. Clearer guidelines would help creators better understand the platform's expectations and reduce the likelihood of accidental violations.

Implement Tiered Enforcement: OnlyFans could adopt a tiered enforcement approach that allows for more graduated responses to policy violations. Rather than immediately removing content or suspending accounts, the platform could issue warnings or temporary content restrictions for minor infractions, giving creators an opportunity to correct their behavior. More serious violations could then be met with stronger penalties. This approach would help ensure that enforcement actions are proportional to the severity of the violation and that creators have a fair chance to rectify their mistakes.

Improve Support for Creators: OnlyFans should enhance the support it provides to creators, particularly those who are new to the platform or who are concerned about complying with guidelines. This could include offering educational resources, such as webinars or tutorials, that explain the platform's policies and best practices for content creation. Additionally, providing access to support representatives who can answer questions and offer guidance on compliance would help creators navigate the platform more confidently.

Foster a More Inclusive Environment: To address concerns about selective enforcement, OnlyFans should work to ensure that its policies are applied consistently across all creators, regardless of their niche, following size, or identity. This could involve regular audits of moderation practices to identify and correct any biases or inconsistencies. By fostering a more inclusive environment, OnlyFans can build greater trust among its creator community and demonstrate its commitment to fairness.

Conclusion: Balancing Policy Enforcement with Creator Autonomy

The effectiveness of OnlyFans' policies is crucial to the platform's long-term success and the well-being of its creators. While the current enforcement mechanisms have helped to establish a safe and legal environment, there are clear areas for improvement in terms of consistency, transparency, and support. By enhancing its moderation practices, providing clearer guidelines, and fostering better communication with creators, OnlyFans can create a more balanced ecosystem where creators feel secure in their ability to produce content while adhering to the platform's standards. These improvements would not only benefit creators but also strengthen the platform's reputation and sustainability in the competitive digital content landscape.

5. Consumer Behavior and Market Dynamics on OnlyFans

The Psychology of Consumer Spending on OnlyFans

Motivations Behind Subscribing to OnlyFans

Desire for Exclusive and Personalized Content: One of the primary motivations for consumers to subscribe to OnlyFans is the access to exclusive and personalized content that is not available on free social media platforms. Subscribers are drawn to the idea of receiving special content that feels tailored to them, whether it's behind-the-scenes footage, intimate conversations, or custom videos. This exclusivity creates a sense of value and belonging, making subscribers feel as though they are part of an inner circle with direct access to the creator.

Connection and Intimacy: OnlyFans offers a level of interaction between creators and subscribers that is more personal than what is typically found on other platforms. Many subscribers are motivated by the opportunity to connect with creators on a deeper level, often developing a sense of intimacy through private messages, personalized shoutouts, and direct interactions. This perceived closeness can be particularly appealing for individuals who seek companionship, validation, or a sense of connection, especially if they are isolated or lonely in their personal lives.

Support for Favorite Creators: Another significant motivator for subscribing to OnlyFans is the desire to support a favorite creator financially. Fans may subscribe to a creator's page as a way of showing appreciation for their work or to help them continue producing content. This patronage model, similar to platforms like Patreon, allows subscribers to feel like they are contributing directly to the creator's success and creative freedom. This motivation is often rooted in a genuine admiration for the creator's talent, personality, or content.

Exploration of Fantasies and Fetishes: For many subscribers, OnlyFans provides a safe and discreet way to explore fantasies and fetishes. The platform allows users to access content that caters to specific interests, often in a more personalized and interactive manner than traditional adult content sites. Subscribers may be motivated by the opportunity to request custom content that aligns with their particular preferences, creating a more engaging and satisfying experience.

Social Proof and FOMO (Fear of Missing Out): Social proof and FOMO also play a role in motivating consumers to subscribe to OnlyFans. When a creator gains popularity and receives attention from others, it can create a bandwagon effect, where potential subscribers feel compelled to join in to avoid missing out on the experience. This is particularly true for creators who generate buzz on social media or in the media, leading to increased curiosity and interest from potential subscribers.

Behavioral Economics Principles Applied to Digital Content Consumption

The Sunk Cost Fallacy: The sunk cost fallacy is a behavioral economics principle that can influence consumer spending on OnlyFans. Once a subscriber has invested time and money into a creator's content, they may feel compelled to continue their subscription, even if they are no longer as interested in the content. The idea that they have already spent money can create a psychological barrier to canceling the subscription, leading to continued spending to avoid the feeling of loss.

Scarcity and Urgency: Scarcity and urgency are powerful tools in driving consumer behavior, and they are often leveraged by creators on OnlyFans to increase subscriptions and sales of pay-per-view (PPV) content. By offering limited-time discounts, exclusive content drops, or time-sensitive offers, creators can create a sense of urgency that prompts subscribers to take immediate action. The fear of missing out on exclusive content or deals can lead to impulsive spending, even if the subscriber had not initially planned to make a purchase.

Anchoring Effect: The anchoring effect, another principle of behavioral economics, refers to the tendency of consumers to rely heavily on the first piece of information they receive when making decisions. On OnlyFans, this can manifest in how creators set their pricing. For example, if a creator sets a high price for a piece of content or a subscription tier, it can create an anchor that makes lower-priced options seem more reasonable by comparison. Subscribers may then be more likely to opt for a mid-tier option because it appears to offer better value relative to the higher-priced alternative.

Mental Accounting: Mental accounting refers to the way consumers categorize and treat money differently depending on its source or intended use. On OnlyFans, subscribers might mentally separate the money they spend on the platform from their other expenditures, viewing it as entertainment or discretionary spending. This mental compartmentalization can lead to less careful consideration of spending decisions, as the money allocated to OnlyFans is perceived differently from funds used for essential expenses.

Commitment Devices: Commitment devices are strategies used by consumers to stick to their spending or behavioral goals. On OnlyFans, creators might offer subscription bundles or longer-term commitments at a discount, encouraging subscribers to commit to multiple months upfront. This tactic leverages the idea that subscribers are more likely to continue engaging with the platform once they've committed financially, reducing the likelihood of churn and ensuring a steady stream of income for the creator.

Impact of Parasocial Relationships on Spending Patterns

Formation of Parasocial Relationships: Parasocial relationships are one-sided relationships where a person feels a strong emotional connection to a media figure who does not reciprocate the relationship. On OnlyFans, these relationships are common, as subscribers often develop a sense of familiarity and emotional attachment to creators through regular interaction and personalized content. The more a subscriber feels connected to a creator, the more likely they are to invest emotionally and financially in the relationship.

Influence on Spending Behavior: Parasocial relationships can significantly impact spending behavior on OnlyFans. Subscribers who feel emotionally connected to a creator are more likely to continue their subscriptions, purchase additional content, and tip generously. This emotional investment can lead to increased spending over time, as subscribers seek to maintain their connection with the creator and support them financially. The desire to please or gain recognition from the creator can also drive spending, particularly in the form of tips or purchasing custom content.

Vulnerability and Exploitation Risks: While parasocial relationships can be harmless and mutually beneficial, they can also create vulnerabilities for subscribers, particularly those who are emotionally or socially isolated. These individuals may become overly dependent on their relationship with the creator, leading to excessive spending or unhealthy attachment. In some cases, creators may unintentionally or deliberately exploit these relationships, encouraging more spending through personalized attention or by creating the illusion of a more reciprocal relationship than actually exists.

Sustaining Parasocial Relationships: Creators on OnlyFans often actively work to sustain parasocial relationships by engaging with subscribers through direct messages, live streams, and personalized content. This ongoing interaction reinforces the subscriber's emotional connection and can lead to a cycle of continued spending. However, maintaining these relationships requires a significant time investment from creators, who must balance the demands of individual subscribers with their broader content production efforts.

Case Study: A subscriber who feels a strong parasocial connection with a popular creator might initially join OnlyFans to access exclusive content. Over time, the subscriber begins to engage more directly with the creator, sending messages and tipping regularly to receive personalized responses. As the emotional connection deepens, the subscriber may start purchasing custom content, despite the increasing financial burden. The creator, recognizing the subscriber's loyalty, might offer special discounts or exclusive offers to encourage further spending, reinforcing the cycle.

Conclusion: Understanding the Complex Dynamics of Consumer Behavior

Consumer behavior on OnlyFans is influenced by a complex interplay of psychological motivations, behavioral economics principles, and the dynamics of parasocial relationships. Understanding these factors is crucial for both creators and subscribers, as they navigate the challenges and opportunities presented by the platform. For creators, leveraging these insights can help build a loyal and engaged audience, while also raising awareness of the ethical considerations involved in fostering parasocial relationships. For subscribers, recognizing the psychological drivers of their spending can lead to more informed and mindful consumption, reducing the risk of over-investment or exploitation. As the platform continues to evolve, the ongoing study of consumer behavior will be key to understanding its impact on both individual users and the broader digital content ecosystem.

Market Dynamics Driving the Race to the Bottom on OnlyFans

Competitive Pressures Among Creators

Intense Competition for Subscribers: The rapid growth of OnlyFans has led to an influx of creators across various niches, all vying for the attention of a limited pool of subscribers. This intense competition drives creators to differentiate themselves, often by offering more content, engaging in more direct interactions, or lowering prices. As more creators enter the platform, the challenge of standing out becomes increasingly difficult, pushing some to resort to more extreme or explicit content to attract and retain subscribers. This environment fosters a race to the bottom, where creators feel compelled to continually escalate their offerings to remain competitive.

Pricing Wars and Undercutting: In an effort to attract more subscribers, some creators engage in pricing wars, offering their content at significantly lower prices than their competitors. This practice of undercutting can lead to a devaluation of content across the platform, as subscribers become accustomed to paying less for more. While lowering prices might lead to a short-term increase in subscriber numbers, it often results in reduced overall earnings per subscriber, forcing creators to rely on volume rather than quality to sustain their income. This cycle of undercutting can pressure creators to produce more content at a lower cost, further contributing to the race to the bottom.

Content Escalation and Boundary Pushing: To stay competitive, creators may feel pressured to push the boundaries of their content, particularly in niches where explicit material is in high demand. As one creator escalates the intensity or explicitness of their content, others may feel compelled to follow suit to avoid losing subscribers. This escalation can lead to a gradual erosion of personal boundaries and ethical standards, as creators produce content that they might not have initially intended to, all in the name of staying relevant and profitable.

Case Study: A fitness influencer on OnlyFans who initially shared workout videos and nutrition tips might find themselves competing with other fitness creators who offer more revealing or provocative content. To keep up, the influencer might start incorporating more suggestive photos or videos, even if it goes against their original brand image. Over time, this escalation could lead to a complete shift in the nature of their content, as they continually adapt to the increasing demands of a highly competitive market.

Economic Forces Shaping Content Trends

Demand for Explicit Content: One of the most powerful economic forces shaping content trends on OnlyFans is the demand for explicit material. Explicit content often commands higher prices, attracts more subscribers, and generates more tips, making it a lucrative option for creators. As a result, many creators who might have initially joined OnlyFans to share non-explicit content find themselves shifting towards more provocative material to capitalize on this demand. This economic incentive creates a feedback loop, where the prevalence of explicit content increases subscriber expectations, further entrenching explicit material as the dominant trend on the platform.

Impact of Pay-Per-View and Tips: The economic model of OnlyFans, which allows creators to earn through pay-per-view (PPV) content and tips, encourages creators to produce content that maximizes these revenue streams. PPV content often includes exclusive or more explicit material that subscribers are willing to pay extra for, while tips are frequently given in response to personalized or interactive content. This model incentivizes creators to focus on content that is most likely to generate immediate financial rewards, often leading to a prioritization of quantity and appeal over quality or creative integrity.

Market Saturation and the Search for Niches: As more creators join OnlyFans, the platform becomes increasingly saturated, making it harder for individual creators to attract and retain subscribers. This market saturation drives creators to explore niche markets where competition might be less intense. However, even within these niches, economic forces can push creators towards commodification, where the unique or specialized content they produce becomes increasingly standardized to meet the broadest possible demand. The pressure to appeal to a wider audience within a niche can lead to the dilution of the niche's uniqueness, contributing to the overall race to the bottom.

Subscription Models and Consumer Expectations: The subscription-based model of OnlyFans also plays a significant role in shaping content trends. Subscribers expect regular updates and new content in exchange for their monthly fees, which can pressure creators to produce content at a rapid pace. This need to continually satisfy subscriber expectations can lead to a focus on volume over quality, as creators rush to meet the demands of a constantly renewing audience. Additionally, as subscribers become accustomed to receiving a certain amount of content for their subscription, creators may feel compelled to offer more for less, further driving down the value of content on the platform.

Case Study: A creator who specializes in cosplay might initially offer high-quality, elaborate costumes and photoshoots. However, as the market becomes more saturated with other cosplay creators, they might feel pressured to produce content more frequently, leading to a decline in the quality of their work. To maintain their income, the creator might start offering more revealing or sexualized versions of their costumes, responding to economic incentives that favor explicit material over artistic expression.

Impact of Market Saturation and Content Commodification

Erosion of Content Value: Market saturation on OnlyFans leads to the commodification of content, where unique or creative offerings become standardized and lose their distinct value. As more creators produce similar types of content, the market becomes flooded with comparable material, reducing the overall perceived value of individual creators' work. This commodification forces creators to compete on price and volume rather than on the uniqueness or quality of their content, leading to a downward spiral where the value of content continues to erode over time.

Subscriber Fatigue and Churn: As content becomes commodified, subscribers may experience fatigue, feeling overwhelmed by the sheer volume of similar content available on the platform. This fatigue can lead to higher churn rates, where subscribers cancel their subscriptions more frequently, either because they no longer see the value in the content or because they are enticed by newer creators offering similar material at lower prices. High churn rates force creators to constantly seek new subscribers to maintain their income, further intensifying the race to the bottom as they compete for attention in an increasingly crowded market.

Diminished Creativity and Risk-Taking: The commodification of content also stifles creativity and risk-taking among creators. When the market rewards standardized content that appeals to the broadest possible audience, creators may become less willing to experiment with new ideas or take creative risks. This focus on safe, formulaic content can lead to a homogenization of material on the platform, where originality and innovation are sacrificed in favor of content that is more likely to generate immediate financial returns. As a result, the diversity and richness of content on OnlyFans may decline, leaving subscribers with fewer truly unique or creative options.

Long-Term Sustainability Concerns: The race to the bottom driven by market saturation and content commodification raises concerns about the long-term sustainability of OnlyFans as a platform. If creators are continually pressured to produce more for less, and if content becomes increasingly devalued, the platform may struggle to retain both creators and subscribers. Creators who feel that their work is no longer valued or that they cannot compete may leave the platform, while subscribers who no longer find the content engaging or worthwhile may seek entertainment elsewhere. This dynamic could ultimately undermine the platform's viability, leading to a loss of diversity and quality in the content ecosystem.

Case Study: An artist who joined OnlyFans to share original artwork and tutorials might find themselves competing with other creators offering similar content. As the market becomes saturated, the artist might feel pressured to lower their prices or increase the frequency of their posts to attract subscribers. Over time, this could lead to a reduction in the quality of their work as they focus on producing more content at a faster pace. Eventually, the artist might find that their unique style has been commodified, blending in with the mass of similar content on the platform.

Conclusion: Navigating the Challenges of Market Dynamics

The market dynamics on OnlyFans, driven by competitive pressures, economic incentives, and market saturation, contribute to a race to the bottom that can erode the value of content, stifle creativity, and threaten the platform's long-term sustainability. Creators must navigate these challenges carefully, balancing the need to remain competitive with the desire to maintain the integrity and quality of their work. For the platform to thrive, it will be essential to foster an environment that rewards originality, supports creators in differentiating themselves, and addresses the pressures that drive content commodification. By understanding and addressing these market dynamics, both creators and the platform can work towards a more sustainable and diverse content ecosystem.

Analysis of the "Simp Economy"

Definition and Origins of the Term "Simp" in the Digital Context

Definition of "Simp": In the digital context, the term "simp" is used to describe someone, typically a man, who is perceived as overly submissive or excessively attentive to someone they are romantically or sexually interested in, often without receiving the same level of attention or affection in return. The term has negative connotations, implying that the "simp" is being manipulated or taken advantage of due to their desire for validation or intimacy. While the term originally surfaced in various online communities, it has since become mainstream, especially on social media platforms like TikTok, Twitter, and Twitch.

Origins and Evolution of the Term: The origins of the term "simp" can be traced back to the 1980s and 1990s, where it was used in hip-hop culture to describe a man who was excessively devoted to a woman, often to his detriment. However, the term gained significant popularity and took on its current digital meaning in the late 2010s, particularly in online gaming and streaming communities. As online platforms like Twitch and OnlyFans grew, so did the use of the term, often in a derogatory manner, to describe men who financially support or give excessive attention to female streamers, influencers, or content creators.

The term "simp" has since evolved to describe a broader range of behaviors, including any form of perceived excessive admiration or financial support towards a creator, especially when it appears one-sided or driven by unrealistic expectations of reciprocity. While the term is often used humorously, it also reflects deeper social dynamics and critiques of gender roles, power imbalances, and the commodification of relationships in the digital age.

Economic and Social Dynamics of Fan-Creator Interactions

The Financial Relationship: In the context of platforms like OnlyFans, the "simp economy" refers to the economic system wherein fans, often labeled as "simps," financially support creators through subscriptions, tips, and purchasing exclusive content. This financial relationship is central to the business model of many digital platforms, where creators rely on the monetary contributions of their most dedicated fans to sustain their income. The willingness of these fans to spend significant amounts of money often stems from a combination of admiration, attraction, and the desire for personal interaction with the creator.

The Role of Parasocial Relationships: The "simp economy" is heavily driven by parasocial relationships—one-sided emotional bonds where the fan feels a deep connection to the creator, despite the relationship being largely transactional or non-reciprocal. These relationships can lead fans to engage in behavior that mimics traditional courtship or romantic interactions, such as giving gifts (in the form of tips or paid content) and seeking the creator's attention and approval. The creators, in turn, often cultivate these relationships by providing personalized content, direct messages, or special shoutouts to their most supportive fans, further reinforcing the fan's emotional investment.

Power Imbalances and Emotional Labor: The dynamic between creators and their "simp" fans is often characterized by significant power imbalances. Creators hold the power to influence and direct fan behavior through the content they produce and the interactions they offer, while fans may feel compelled to continue supporting the creator in hopes of receiving more attention or validation. This dynamic can place considerable emotional labor on creators, who must manage these relationships carefully to maintain their income without crossing ethical boundaries or exploiting their fans.

Case Study: Consider a popular female creator on OnlyFans who has built a significant following through a mix of lifestyle content and personalized interactions. Over time, a subset of her fans begins to stand out as particularly devoted, regularly tipping large amounts and purchasing all of her exclusive content. These fans, often labeled as "simps" by their peers, develop a strong emotional attachment to the creator, frequently messaging her and requesting custom content. The creator, recognizing the financial benefit of these relationships, might offer these fans special treatment, such as personalized responses or exclusive live chats, further deepening their emotional investment.

Social Stigma and Criticism: The "simp economy" is often subject to social stigma and criticism, particularly from those who view the behavior of "simps" as misguided or degrading. Critics argue that these fans are being exploited by creators who offer only minimal interaction in return for significant financial support. On the other hand, some defend the "simp" behavior, arguing that it is a form of entertainment or self-expression that provides value to the fan, even if the relationship is largely one-sided. The debate around the "simp economy" reflects broader societal concerns about the commodification of relationships and the ethical implications of digital fan-creator dynamics.

Long-term Implications for Consumer Behavior and Platform Sustainability

Consumer Behavior and Spending Patterns: The "simp economy" has significant implications for consumer behavior on platforms like OnlyFans. Fans who engage deeply in parasocial relationships may develop spending patterns that prioritize emotional connection over financial prudence, leading to potentially excessive or unsustainable spending. The emotional attachment to a creator can drive repeat spending, as fans continually seek out new ways to interact or gain the creator's attention. Over time, this behavior can lead to financial strain for some fans, particularly if they are spending beyond their means to maintain the perceived relationship.

Platform Sustainability: For platforms like OnlyFans, the "simp economy" represents both an opportunity and a challenge. On the one hand, the financial contributions of highly engaged fans are crucial to the platform's revenue model, providing a steady stream of income for creators and, by extension, the platform itself. However, the reliance on a small number of highly invested fans also raises concerns about the sustainability of this model. If these fans begin to experience burnout or financial difficulties, they may reduce their spending or leave the platform altogether, potentially destabilizing the income of the creators who rely on them.

Ethical Considerations and Platform Responsibility: The long-term viability of the "simp economy" also raises important ethical considerations for platforms like OnlyFans. As the line between genuine fan support and exploitation becomes increasingly blurred, platforms may face pressure to implement policies that protect both creators and fans. This could include measures to prevent financial exploitation, such as spending limits, as well as tools to help creators manage the emotional labor involved in maintaining parasocial relationships. Ensuring that the platform fosters healthy, sustainable interactions between creators and fans is essential for maintaining trust and long-term engagement.

Changing Market Dynamics: As the "simp economy" continues to evolve, it may also influence broader market dynamics on digital platforms. The emphasis on personalized interaction and emotional connection could lead to a greater focus on niche content and smaller, more dedicated fan bases, rather than mass appeal. This shift could encourage creators to cultivate more meaningful relationships with a smaller number of highly engaged fans, rather than pursuing large, generalized audiences. However, this approach also comes with risks, as it increases creators' dependence on a small group of fans, making them more vulnerable to fluctuations in support.

Case Study: A creator who has built their income largely on the financial contributions of a few "simp" fans may find themselves in a precarious position if those fans decide to reduce their spending or leave the platform. This reliance on a small number of high-spending fans can make the creator's income volatile and unsustainable in the long term. To mitigate this risk, the creator might choose to diversify their content offerings or expand their audience base, reducing their dependence on any one group of fans and ensuring a more stable income stream.

Conclusion: Navigating the Complexities of the Simp Economy

The "simp economy" on platforms like OnlyFans is a complex and multifaceted phenomenon that reflects deeper economic, social, and ethical dynamics in the digital age. While it offers significant financial opportunities for creators, it also presents challenges related to consumer behavior, platform sustainability, and ethical considerations. As the digital content landscape continues to evolve, it will be important for both creators and platforms to navigate these dynamics carefully, ensuring that the relationships between fans and creators remain healthy, sustainable, and mutually beneficial. Understanding the long-term implications of the "simp economy" will be key to fostering a content ecosystem that is both profitable and ethically sound.

6. Case Studies of Influencers on OnlyFans: Profiles of Top-Earning Creators

Detailed Analysis of Successful Creator Strategies

Case Study 1: Belle Delphine

Background: Belle Delphine is a British social media influencer and cosplayer who gained widespread fame through her provocative and often controversial content. Before joining OnlyFans, she built a large following on platforms like Instagram and YouTube, where she combined cosplay with suggestive humor, often blurring the lines between parody and adult content. Her pre-existing fame and unique brand positioned her for immediate success when she transitioned to OnlyFans.

Strategy: Belle Delphine's success on OnlyFans is largely attributed to her ability to leverage her established online persona. She uses a combination of high-quality cosplay, adult content, and playful, often satirical marketing to engage her audience. Delphine is known for creating viral moments that generate significant media attention, such as selling her "GamerGirl Bath Water," which further drives traffic to her OnlyFans page.

Her strategy also includes creating a sense of exclusivity and scarcity by offering limited-time content and engaging directly with her subscribers through personalized messages and custom content. This approach not only retains subscribers but also encourages higher spending through tips and pay-per-view (PPV) content. Delphine's ability to create a strong brand identity and cultivate a dedicated fanbase has been key to her success.

Key Takeaways:

- Leveraging pre-existing fame and a strong online persona can significantly boost success on OnlyFans.

- Viral marketing and creating buzz around unique or controversial content can drive traffic and engagement.

- Personal interaction with subscribers and offering exclusive content helps build loyalty and increase revenue.

Case Study 2: Cardi B

Background: Cardi B, a Grammy-winning rapper and media personality, joined OnlyFans in 2020. Unlike many other creators on the platform, Cardi B does not primarily use OnlyFans to share explicit content. Instead, she offers behind-the-scenes footage, personal insights, and direct interaction with her fans. Her presence on the platform is part of a broader strategy to engage more closely with her audience and provide content that fans can't find elsewhere.

Strategy: Cardi B's success on OnlyFans is rooted in her ability to leverage her existing celebrity status to create an exclusive space for her fans. She uses the platform to share unfiltered content, including behind-the-scenes footage from her music videos, personal vlogs, and discussions about her life and career. By offering content that feels more personal and direct than what she shares on other social media platforms, Cardi B has been able to maintain a large and loyal subscriber base.

Additionally, Cardi B uses OnlyFans to interact directly with her fans, answering questions and responding to comments, which fosters a strong sense of community and connection. Her strategy is less about volume and more about providing value through authenticity and exclusivity. This approach has allowed her to maintain high subscription numbers without relying on the explicit content that dominates the platform.

Key Takeaways:

- Leveraging celebrity status can draw significant attention and subscribers without relying on explicit content.

- Offering personal, behind-the-scenes content can create a sense of intimacy and exclusivity that attracts and retains subscribers.

- Direct interaction with fans enhances the sense of community and increases subscriber loyalty.

Case Study 3: Mia Khalifa

Background: Mia Khalifa is a former adult film actress who has since transitioned to being a social media personality and sports commentator. Khalifa joined OnlyFans to take control of her own content and monetize her large following while moving away from the adult industry. Her presence on the platform is focused on sharing lifestyle content, personal insights, and occasionally risqué material, though she has made it clear that she is no longer involved in explicit adult content.

Strategy: Mia Khalifa's strategy on OnlyFans is centered around rebranding herself and distancing her current work from her past in the adult industry. She uses the platform to share content related to her personal life, fitness routines, and her journey in moving beyond her past career. Khalifa's openness about her struggles and her efforts to reclaim her narrative have resonated with her audience, building a community of supportive fans.

Khalifa also capitalizes on the platform's flexibility by offering personalized content, such as custom videos and direct messaging, which provides an additional revenue stream. Her strategy includes being transparent about her experiences and engaging with her fans in a way that feels authentic and empowering, which helps her stand out on a platform often associated with more explicit content.

Key Takeaways:

- Rebranding and using OnlyFans as a platform for personal storytelling can attract a dedicated audience.

- Transparency and authenticity in content can build strong connections with subscribers, fostering loyalty.

- Diversifying content offerings, such as custom videos and personalized messages, can increase revenue streams.

Common Traits and Practices Among Top Earners

1. Strong Pre-existing Fanbase: Top earners on OnlyFans often start with a significant following on other social media platforms. Having a strong pre-existing fanbase allows creators to quickly build a subscriber base on OnlyFans, leveraging their existing brand and reputation.

2. Unique and Authentic Branding: Successful creators often have a unique and consistent brand that distinguishes them from others on the platform. Whether it's through a specific niche, personality, or content style, top earners create a brand identity that resonates with their audience and attracts subscribers who are willing to pay for exclusive access.

3. Personal Interaction and Custom Content: Many top earners emphasize direct interaction with their subscribers, offering personalized content such as custom videos, private messages, and one-on-one chats. This personal touch not only increases engagement but also encourages higher spending through tips and PPV content.

4. Content Exclusivity and Scarcity: Creating a sense of exclusivity or scarcity is a common strategy among top earners. By offering limited-time content, exclusive material, or early access to certain posts, creators can drive subscriber interest and urgency, leading to increased subscriptions and purchases.

5. Strategic Pricing and Promotions: Top earners often use strategic pricing to maximize their revenue. This can include offering discounts for longer-term subscriptions, bundling content, or using tiered pricing to cater to different levels of subscriber engagement. Promotions and limited-time offers are also effective in attracting new subscribers and encouraging existing ones to spend more.

Lessons from Their Growth Trajectories and Business Models

1. Diversification of Revenue Streams: One key lesson from top earners is the importance of diversifying revenue streams. While subscriptions provide a steady income, many successful creators also earn significant revenue through PPV content, tips, and custom requests. By offering multiple ways for fans to support them, creators can maximize their earnings and reduce their reliance on any single revenue source.

2. Adaptability and Innovation: The digital content landscape is constantly evolving, and top earners demonstrate the importance of adaptability and innovation. Whether it's responding to changing platform policies, shifting audience preferences, or exploring new content formats, successful creators are those who continuously evolve their strategies to stay relevant and engaged with their audience.

3. Building and Maintaining Community: The most successful creators on OnlyFans understand the value of building and maintaining a strong community. By fostering a sense of belonging and engagement among their subscribers, these creators create a loyal fanbase that supports them over the long term. Community-building strategies include regular communication, rewarding loyal subscribers with exclusive content, and creating interactive experiences such as live streams or Q&A sessions.

4. Balancing Personal and Professional Boundaries: While personal interaction is a key component of success on OnlyFans, top earners also understand the importance of maintaining boundaries. Balancing personal life with professional content creation is crucial for long-term sustainability, and successful creators set clear boundaries to protect their mental health and avoid burnout.

5. Ethical Considerations and Transparency: Finally, ethical considerations and transparency play a significant role in the success of top creators. Being transparent with subscribers about the nature of their content, their boundaries, and the realities of their work helps build trust and respect. This transparency, combined with ethical practices in content creation and subscriber interaction, contributes to a sustainable and positive relationship with their audience.

Conclusion: Insights from Top-Earning Creators

The success of top earners on OnlyFans is driven by a combination of strong branding, strategic content creation, and effective audience engagement. By analyzing the strategies of these creators, aspiring influencers can learn valuable lessons about building a sustainable and profitable presence on the platform. Key takeaways include the importance of leveraging an existing fanbase, maintaining authenticity, diversifying revenue streams, and balancing personal interaction with professional boundaries. As the digital content landscape continues to evolve, these insights will be crucial for navigating the challenges and opportunities presented by platforms like OnlyFans.

Examination of Content Strategies and Their Impact

Innovative Approaches to Content Creation

1. Niche Content Specialization: One of the most innovative approaches to content creation on OnlyFans is the focus on niche content. Creators who identify and cater to specific interests or communities often find success by offering content that is tailored to a particular audience. This could range from cosplay and fetish content to fitness routines, educational tutorials, or even mental health advocacy. By targeting a niche market, creators can build a loyal following that values the uniqueness and specificity of their content, reducing direct competition and increasing subscriber retention.

Case Study: A creator specializing in eco-friendly living and sustainability tips might attract subscribers who are passionate about the environment. By offering content such as zero-waste lifestyle guides, DIY tutorials, and eco-conscious product reviews, the creator can carve out a niche that appeals to a specific demographic, leading to a dedicated and engaged subscriber base.

2. Interactive and Personalized Content: Another innovative strategy is the use of interactive and personalized content to engage subscribers. This approach includes live streams, Q&A sessions, polls, and custom content requests that allow subscribers to interact directly with the creator. Personalization not only enhances the subscriber experience but also creates a sense of exclusivity and connection, encouraging higher levels of engagement and spending.

Case Study: A fitness trainer on OnlyFans might offer personalized workout plans and nutrition advice tailored to individual subscribers. By providing one-on-one consultations and feedback, the trainer can create a more interactive and value-driven experience, which can justify higher subscription fees and foster long-term subscriber loyalty.

3. Multi-Platform Content Integration: Successful creators often integrate their OnlyFans content with other social media platforms to create a cohesive brand presence. By using platforms like Instagram, TikTok, Twitter, and YouTube, creators can reach a broader audience and drive traffic to their OnlyFans page. Cross-promotion of content across multiple platforms helps build brand awareness, attract new subscribers, and maintain engagement with existing followers.

Case Study: A creator who is also active on Instagram might use the platform to share behind-the-scenes photos and teaser clips that link back to exclusive content on OnlyFans. This strategy not only broadens the creator's reach but also encourages followers from other platforms to subscribe for more in-depth or exclusive material.

4. Episodic Content and Storytelling: Episodic content and storytelling are innovative ways to keep subscribers engaged over time. By creating a series of interconnected posts or videos that build upon each other, creators can generate anticipation and encourage subscribers to stay subscribed to see how the story unfolds. This approach is particularly effective in niches like adult content, cosplay, and lifestyle vlogging, where narratives can be used to deepen the connection between the creator and their audience.

Case Study: A creator might develop a series of themed photo shoots or videos that follow a narrative arc, such as a fantasy cosplay adventure or a fitness transformation journey. By releasing episodes periodically, the creator keeps subscribers coming back for more, while also creating opportunities for cross-promotion and upselling additional content related to the series.

Use of Marketing, Branding, and Social Media to Drive Subscriptions

1. Strategic Use of Social Media: Social media platforms are essential tools for marketing and branding in the OnlyFans ecosystem. Creators use social media to build their personal brand, promote their OnlyFans content, and engage with potential subscribers. By consistently posting relevant, high-quality content on platforms like Instagram, TikTok, and Twitter, creators can drive traffic to their OnlyFans page and convert followers into paying subscribers.

Case Study: A creator might use TikTok to post short, engaging videos that highlight their personality and showcase snippets of the content available on OnlyFans. By using trending hashtags, collaborating with other influencers, and engaging with their audience through comments and duets, the creator can increase visibility and attract new subscribers to their OnlyFans account.

2. Branding Consistency and Aesthetic: A strong and consistent brand is crucial for success on OnlyFans. Creators who establish a clear aesthetic, tone, and message across all their platforms are more likely to build a recognizable and trusted brand. Consistency in branding helps create a cohesive identity that resonates with the target audience, making it easier to attract and retain subscribers.

Case Study: A creator with a focus on luxury lifestyle content might use a consistent color palette, high-quality photography, and polished, aspirational messaging across their OnlyFans, Instagram, and website. This cohesive branding reinforces the creator's image as a luxury lifestyle influencer, attracting subscribers who are interested in premium, exclusive content.

3. Leveraging Collaborations and Cross-Promotions: Collaborations with other creators and cross-promotions are effective marketing strategies that help expand reach and attract new subscribers. By teaming up with creators who have complementary audiences, influencers can tap into new fan bases and offer joint content that appeals to a broader audience. Cross-promotions, such as shoutouts or joint live streams, also provide added value to subscribers, who may be more inclined to subscribe to multiple creators offering collaborative content.

Case Study: Two fitness influencers on OnlyFans might collaborate on a joint workout series, where each influencer shares a different part of the routine. By promoting each other's content to their respective audiences, they can attract new subscribers who are interested in the full series and benefit from the added value of a collaborative offering.

4. Utilizing Promotions and Limited-Time Offers: Promotional tactics, such as discounts, limited-time offers, and free trials, are powerful tools for driving subscriptions on OnlyFans. Creators often use these promotions to attract new subscribers, encourage upgrades to higher-priced tiers, or re-engage former subscribers. Limited-time offers create a sense of urgency, prompting potential subscribers to act quickly to take advantage of the deal.

Case Study: A creator might offer a 50% discount on their monthly subscription fee for the first week of a new content series launch. This promotion could attract new subscribers who are curious about the series and incentivize them to continue their subscription at the regular price once they've seen the value of the content.

Ethical Considerations and Their Impact on Success

1. Transparency and Authenticity: Transparency and authenticity are key ethical considerations that can significantly impact a creator's success on OnlyFans. Subscribers value honesty and genuine interaction, and creators who are transparent about their content, boundaries, and expectations are more likely to build trust and long-term relationships with their audience. This transparency includes being upfront about what subscribers can expect from different tiers, how often content will be posted, and the nature of interactions (e.g., direct messaging, custom content).

Case Study: A creator who is transparent about their content boundaries—such as clearly stating what types of content they do or do not offer—can avoid misunderstandings and maintain a positive relationship with their subscribers. This honesty fosters trust and respect, leading to higher subscriber retention and a more loyal fan base.

2. Ethical Management of Parasocial Relationships: Creators on OnlyFans often navigate parasocial relationships, where fans feel a deep connection to the creator despite the relationship being one-sided. Managing these relationships ethically involves setting clear boundaries, avoiding manipulation, and ensuring that interactions remain respectful and professional. Creators who prioritize the well-being of their subscribers and avoid exploiting these relationships are more likely to maintain a positive reputation and long-term success.

Case Study: A creator who receives a high volume of personal messages from subscribers might choose to set boundaries by limiting the number of custom content requests or offering scheduled Q&A sessions instead of continuous one-on-one interactions. By managing these relationships ethically, the creator maintains their mental health and ensures that their subscribers feel valued without fostering unrealistic expectations.

3. Respect for Privacy and Consent: Respecting privacy and ensuring informed consent are critical ethical considerations on OnlyFans. Creators must be diligent in protecting their own privacy as well as that of their subscribers. This includes taking precautions to prevent doxxing, safeguarding personal information, and ensuring that all parties involved in content creation (e.g., collaborators) have given explicit consent. Respecting these ethical principles is not only important for legal compliance but also for maintaining trust with subscribers.

Case Study: A creator who collaborates with others might use contracts and consent forms to ensure that all parties agree to the terms of the content creation and distribution. This practice protects both the creator and their collaborators, reinforcing the importance of ethical standards in the content creation process.

4. Avoiding Exploitative Practices: Successful creators often navigate the ethical line between monetizing their content and avoiding exploitative practices. This includes being mindful of pricing, not pressuring subscribers into spending more than they are comfortable with, and offering value that aligns with the subscription cost. Creators who prioritize ethical practices are more likely to build a sustainable and respectful relationship with their audience, leading to long-term success.

Case Study: A creator who offers custom content might set clear guidelines on pricing and turnaround times, avoiding upselling tactics that pressure subscribers into spending beyond their means. By providing consistent value and respecting subscribers' financial boundaries, the creator fosters a positive and ethical relationship with their audience.

Conclusion: Balancing Innovation with Ethical Considerations

The success of content strategies on OnlyFans is influenced by a combination of innovative approaches to content creation, effective marketing and branding, and a commitment to ethical practices. Creators who embrace niche specialization, interactive content, and multi-platform integration are well-positioned to attract and retain subscribers. However, these strategies must be balanced with ethical considerations, such as transparency, privacy, and the respectful management of fan relationships. By aligning innovative content strategies with ethical principles, creators can build a sustainable and successful presence on OnlyFans, fostering trust and loyalty among their subscribers.

Lessons Learned from Successful and Controversial Influencers

Key Takeaways from Creators Who Navigated Ethical Challenges

1. The Importance of Transparency and Communication:

One of the most crucial lessons from successful creators is the value of transparency and open communication with their audience. Creators who clearly communicate their content boundaries, pricing structures, and what subscribers can expect are more likely to build trust and maintain long-term relationships with their audience. This transparency not only helps set realistic expectations but also reduces the likelihood of misunderstandings or disappointment.

Case Study: A creator who specializes in non-explicit lifestyle content might face pressure from subscribers requesting more provocative material. By openly discussing their content limits and the type of content they are comfortable producing, the creator can maintain their integrity while managing subscriber expectations. This approach also helps filter their audience, attracting subscribers who genuinely appreciate the content they offer.

Key Takeaway: Clear communication and transparency foster trust and respect between creators and their audience, leading to higher subscriber satisfaction and retention.

2. Balancing Personal Boundaries with Audience Engagement:

Successful creators often find a balance between engaging with their audience and maintaining personal boundaries. While interaction and personalization are key drivers of subscriber loyalty, it's essential for creators to set limits that protect their mental health and well-being. This balance ensures that creators can sustain their content creation efforts over the long term without experiencing burnout.

Case Study: A creator who regularly engages with subscribers through direct messaging and live streams might establish specific hours or days for these interactions, allowing them to recharge and focus on content creation during other times. This structured approach helps prevent overcommitment and ensures that the creator can continue offering high-quality content without compromising their personal well-being.

Key Takeaway: Setting and maintaining personal boundaries is essential for long-term sustainability and mental health, allowing creators to engage with their audience without experiencing burnout.

3. Ethical Monetization Strategies:

Navigating the fine line between monetization and exploitation is a key ethical challenge for creators. Those who prioritize ethical monetization strategies—such as fair pricing, avoiding manipulative upselling, and offering genuine value for money—tend to build stronger, more loyal audiences. Ethical creators understand that long-term success depends on maintaining a positive and respectful relationship with their subscribers.

Case Study: A creator might offer tiered subscription levels that provide varying degrees of access and content without pressuring subscribers to opt for the highest tier. By ensuring that each tier offers fair value for its cost, the creator builds trust and encourages voluntary upgrades rather than coercive spending.

Key Takeaway: Ethical monetization practices build trust and encourage long-term subscriber loyalty, which is more sustainable than short-term profit maximization through manipulative tactics.

Analysis of Controversial Incidents and Their Outcomes

1. The Bella Thorne Controversy:

Incident: In August 2020, actress Bella Thorne joined OnlyFans and reportedly earned over $1 million within 24 hours. However, her presence on the platform sparked controversy when she was accused of misleading subscribers by promising explicit content that was never delivered. The backlash led to OnlyFans implementing policy changes, including capping the price of pay-per-view content and limiting the amount creators could receive in tips.

Outcome: Thorne's actions had a significant impact on the platform, particularly for smaller creators who faced reduced earning potential due to the new restrictions. The incident highlighted the importance of managing expectations and the potential consequences of misleading marketing practices.

Lessons Learned:

- Creators must be transparent and honest in their marketing to avoid misleading their audience.

- High-profile controversies can lead to platform-wide changes that affect all creators, underscoring the need for responsible behavior by influencers with large followings.

2. The Mia Khalifa Rebranding Effort:

Incident: Mia Khalifa, a former adult film actress, faced significant challenges in rebranding herself after leaving the adult industry. Her efforts to distance herself from her past and focus on new content on platforms like OnlyFans were met with mixed reactions, as she continued to grapple with the stigma and exploitation associated with her previous career.

Outcome: Khalifa's rebranding efforts, while challenging, have been largely successful in reshaping her public image. She has used platforms like OnlyFans to share personal stories, lifestyle content, and advocacy work, gradually shifting the narrative around her identity.

Lessons Learned:

- Rebranding requires consistent effort, transparency, and a commitment to new content that aligns with the creator's current values and goals.

- Creators can successfully navigate past controversies by staying true to their evolving identity and engaging with their audience in a meaningful, authentic way.

3. The Austin McBroom and ACE Family Controversy:

Incident: Austin McBroom, a member of the popular YouTube family channel "The ACE Family," faced backlash after allegations of inappropriate behavior and exploitation of fans surfaced. The controversy extended to their use of OnlyFans, where fans accused them of overcharging for content and failing to deliver promised value.

Outcome: The controversy damaged the ACE Family's reputation and led to a decline in their subscriber base. It also sparked broader discussions about the ethics of family influencers monetizing their content, particularly when involving their children.

Lessons Learned:

- Ethical considerations are especially important when family members, particularly children, are involved in content creation.

- Exploiting fan loyalty for financial gain can lead to significant reputational damage and loss of trust, which can be difficult to rebuild.

Best Practices for Balancing Success with Ethical Content Creation

1. Prioritize Authenticity and Transparency: Creators should be clear and honest about what they offer, avoiding misleading marketing or exaggerated claims. Transparency not only builds trust but also sets realistic expectations, reducing the likelihood of subscriber dissatisfaction.

2. Respect Subscriber Boundaries and Privacy: Creators must respect the privacy and boundaries of their subscribers, ensuring that interactions remain professional and consensual. This includes managing parasocial relationships ethically and avoiding exploitative practices.

3. Set and Communicate Clear Boundaries: To prevent burnout and maintain personal well-being, creators should set clear boundaries regarding their availability and the type of content they produce. Communicating these boundaries to subscribers helps manage expectations and fosters a respectful relationship.

4. Offer Fair Value for Money: Creators should ensure that their pricing reflects the value of the content they provide. Ethical monetization involves offering a range of options that cater to different levels of engagement, without pressuring subscribers to spend more than they are comfortable with.

5. Engage with the Community Responsibly: Creators who engage with their audience should do so in a way that fosters a positive and inclusive community. This includes addressing controversies transparently, apologizing for mistakes, and taking corrective action when necessary.

6. Stay Informed and Adapt to Changes: The digital content landscape is constantly evolving, and creators must stay informed about platform policies, industry trends, and audience preferences. Adapting to these changes while maintaining ethical standards is key to long-term success.

Conclusion: Learning from Success and Controversy

The experiences of successful and controversial influencers on platforms like OnlyFans offer valuable lessons for content creators. By prioritizing transparency, ethical monetization, and respectful engagement, creators can build sustainable careers while maintaining the trust and loyalty of their audience. Controversial incidents highlight the potential risks of unethical behavior, underscoring the importance of responsible content creation in the digital age. By balancing success with ethical practices, creators can navigate the complexities of the online content ecosystem and achieve long-term growth and sustainability.

7. Strategies for Ethical Content Creation

Best Practices for Maintaining Content Quality

1. Guidelines for Producing High-Quality, Engaging Content

Understand Your Audience: The foundation of high-quality content creation is a deep understanding of your audience. Creators should regularly engage with their subscribers to learn about their preferences, interests, and expectations. This feedback can be gathered through direct messages, polls, and comments, allowing creators to tailor their content to meet subscriber needs.

Focus on Consistency and Regular Updates: Consistency is key to maintaining subscriber interest and engagement. Creators should establish a content schedule that works for them and stick to it. Whether it's weekly posts, bi-weekly updates, or monthly themed content drops, consistency helps build anticipation and keeps subscribers engaged.

Invest in Production Quality: High-quality visuals, clear audio, and professional editing can significantly enhance the appeal of content. Creators should consider investing in good equipment, such as a high-resolution camera, microphone, and lighting setup, to produce content that stands out. Additionally, learning basic editing skills or using professional editing services can help polish content and make it more visually appealing.

Create a Unique Brand Aesthetic: A strong and consistent aesthetic helps build a recognizable brand. Creators should develop a visual style and tone that reflects their personality and resonates with their audience. This could include consistent use of colors, fonts, and themes across all content, as well as maintaining a cohesive narrative or message that aligns with the creator's brand identity.

Experiment and Innovate: To keep content fresh and engaging, creators should not be afraid to experiment with new ideas, formats, and themes. Innovation can involve trying out new content types, such as interactive polls, live streams, or behind-the-scenes footage, or exploring different creative directions that push the boundaries of their usual style.

Prioritize Authenticity: Authenticity is crucial for building trust and loyalty among subscribers. Creators should focus on being genuine and true to their values, rather than producing content solely based on what they think will sell. Authenticity resonates with audiences and helps create deeper connections.

2. Strategies for Diversifying Content Types and Revenue Streams

Expand Content Offerings: Diversifying content types can help attract a wider audience and keep existing subscribers engaged. Creators can expand their offerings by including a mix of content such as tutorials, vlogs, Q&A sessions, podcasts, or even downloadable resources like eBooks or guides. This variety ensures that there is something for everyone and keeps the content fresh.

Leverage Tiered Subscription Models: Offering tiered subscription levels allows creators to cater to different segments of their audience. Each tier can provide varying levels of access and exclusive content, such as early access to posts, behind-the-scenes material, or personalized interactions. This approach not only maximizes revenue but also provides value at different price points.

Explore Pay-Per-View and Custom Content: In addition to subscription-based content, creators can offer pay-per-view (PPV) content and custom requests as additional revenue streams. PPV content might include exclusive videos, special event coverage, or limited-time offers, while custom content allows subscribers to request personalized material for a premium price. These options give subscribers more ways to engage with the creator and support their work.

Offer Merchandise and Digital Products: Creators can diversify their revenue streams by selling branded merchandise, such as clothing, accessories, or home decor, as well as digital products like eBooks, courses, or exclusive digital art. Merchandise not only generates additional income but also strengthens the creator's brand by allowing fans to feel more connected.

Collaborate with Other Creators: Collaborations with other creators can introduce your content to new audiences and provide fresh perspectives. Joint projects, co-hosted events, or collaborative series can bring added value to subscribers and open up new revenue opportunities. Collaborations also encourage cross-promotion, which can boost visibility and attract new subscribers.

Monetize Through Sponsorships and Partnerships: As a creator's influence grows, they may attract sponsorship deals or partnerships with brands that align with their content and values. Sponsored posts, product placements, or brand collaborations can provide significant revenue, provided they are executed transparently and ethically. It's important to choose partnerships that resonate with the audience and maintain the creator's authenticity.

3. Tips for Maintaining a Professional and Ethical Approach

Set Clear Boundaries and Expectations: Maintaining professionalism involves setting clear boundaries with subscribers regarding content, communication, and interactions. Creators should communicate their limits upfront and ensure that all interactions are respectful and appropriate. This helps prevent misunderstandings and ensures that the relationship between the creator and subscribers remains healthy and sustainable.

Prioritize Consent and Privacy: Creators must respect the privacy and consent of everyone involved in their content. This includes obtaining explicit consent from collaborators, protecting the privacy of subscribers, and ensuring that personal information is safeguarded. Ethical content creation also involves being mindful of the potential impact of content on others and taking steps to minimize any harm.

Stay Informed About Platform Policies: Understanding and adhering to the platform's terms of service and content guidelines is crucial for maintaining a professional presence. Creators should stay updated on any policy changes and ensure that their content complies with all rules and regulations. This not only protects the creator from potential penalties but also ensures that they are operating within ethical boundaries.

Be Transparent About Monetization: Transparency in monetization practices builds trust with subscribers. Creators should clearly communicate the value offered at different subscription levels, explain the nature of any sponsored content, and avoid deceptive marketing practices. Being upfront about monetization strategies helps manage subscriber expectations and fosters a positive relationship.

Engage with Your Audience Responsibly: Responsible engagement involves interacting with subscribers in a way that is respectful, inclusive, and supportive. Creators should be mindful of the power dynamics at play in parasocial relationships and avoid exploiting subscribers' emotional investments. Ethical creators prioritize the well-being of their audience and engage in a manner that promotes a positive community environment.

Commit to Continuous Learning and Improvement: The digital content landscape is constantly evolving, and creators should commit to continuous learning and improvement. This includes staying informed about industry trends, honing content creation skills, and reflecting on ethical practices. By continuously striving to improve, creators can maintain a professional and ethical approach that supports long-term success.

Conclusion: Balancing Quality, Innovation, and Ethics

Maintaining high-quality, engaging content while upholding ethical standards is essential for long-term success in content creation. By understanding their audience, diversifying content offerings, and adhering to ethical practices, creators can build a sustainable and respected brand. These strategies not only enhance the creator's reputation but also contribute to a positive and supportive online community, fostering trust and loyalty among subscribers. As the digital landscape continues to evolve, creators who prioritize quality, innovation, and ethics will be well-positioned to thrive.

Balancing Profitability with Ethical Considerations

Methods for Achieving Financial Goals Without Compromising Values

1. Implementing Value-Based Pricing: Value-based pricing involves setting prices that reflect the true worth of the content or services offered while aligning with the creator's values. Rather than undercutting competitors or relying on high-pressure sales tactics, creators can focus on offering content that genuinely provides value to subscribers. This approach ensures that pricing is fair and justifiable, fostering trust and long-term loyalty among the audience.

Example: A creator who offers educational content might set tiered pricing based on the depth and exclusivity of the material. The base tier could include general content accessible to all subscribers, while higher tiers offer in-depth tutorials, personalized feedback, or one-on-one consultations. By aligning pricing with the value provided, the creator can achieve financial goals while maintaining ethical standards.

2. Diversifying Income Streams Ethically: Diversifying income streams is a key strategy for achieving financial stability without resorting to unethical practices. Creators can explore various monetization options, such as offering premium content, merchandise, custom services, or affiliate marketing, while ensuring that each revenue stream aligns with their values and provides clear value to their audience.

Example: A creator who focuses on wellness might offer digital products such as eBooks or guided meditation sessions, alongside subscription content on OnlyFans. By providing a range of products that cater to different aspects of their audience's needs, the creator can increase their income without compromising their integrity or the quality of their primary content.

3. Setting and Communicating Clear Boundaries: To maintain both profitability and ethical integrity, creators must set clear boundaries regarding the content they are willing to produce and the interactions they engage in with subscribers. Communicating these boundaries upfront helps manage expectations and prevents situations where the creator might feel pressured to compromise their values for financial gain.

Example: A creator might make it clear that while they offer personalized content, they will not produce explicit material or engage in certain types of interactions. By clearly stating these boundaries in their profile and marketing materials, the creator attracts an audience that respects their limits, reducing the pressure to compromise their values.

4. Engaging in Ethical Marketing Practices: Ethical marketing involves promoting content in a way that is honest, transparent, and respectful of the audience. This includes avoiding clickbait, being clear about what subscribers will receive, and not exaggerating the value or exclusivity of the content. Ethical marketing builds trust and attracts subscribers who value integrity, leading to a more sustainable and loyal fanbase.

Example: A creator might use social media to share snippets of their content with clear descriptions of what is included in each subscription tier. They avoid making false promises or implying that content is more exclusive than it actually is. This approach ensures that subscribers know exactly what they are paying for, reducing dissatisfaction and fostering a positive relationship.

5. Fostering a Supportive Community: Building a community around shared values and interests can enhance both profitability and ethical integrity. A supportive community encourages engagement, loyalty, and mutual respect, creating an environment where subscribers feel valued and connected. This sense of community can lead to higher retention rates and organic growth through word-of-mouth.

Example: A creator might host regular live Q&A sessions where subscribers can discuss topics related to the content and share their experiences. By fostering open dialogue and creating a space for mutual support, the creator builds a strong community that is more likely to remain loyal and actively promote the content to others.

Case Studies of Creators Who Successfully Balanced Both

1. Amanda Lee (Fitness and Wellness Influencer)

Background: Amanda Lee, a fitness and wellness influencer, has built a successful brand by offering workout plans, nutrition advice, and mental wellness content across multiple platforms, including OnlyFans. Amanda's approach focuses on promoting a healthy lifestyle and positive body image, while maintaining a strong commitment to ethical practices.

Strategy: Amanda Lee's success lies in her ability to balance profitability with ethical content creation. She offers tiered subscription options that cater to different levels of commitment, from basic workout plans to personalized coaching. Amanda is transparent about her content, ensuring that subscribers know what to expect at each level. She avoids promoting unrealistic body standards or engaging in deceptive marketing, instead focusing on authenticity and evidence-based advice.

Outcome: Amanda Lee's ethical approach has earned her a loyal following that appreciates her honesty and the quality of her content. By aligning her financial goals with her values, she has built a sustainable business that supports both her subscribers' well-being and her own professional integrity.

2. Casey Zander (Relationship and Personal Development Coach)

Background: Casey Zander is a relationship and personal development coach who uses OnlyFans as a platform to offer advice, courses, and personalized coaching sessions. His content focuses on helping individuals build healthier relationships and develop personal confidence, all while adhering to a strict ethical code.

Strategy: Casey Zander's approach to content creation involves setting clear boundaries around the types of interactions and advice he provides. He is transparent about the limitations of his coaching and avoids making exaggerated claims about the effectiveness of his methods. Casey also uses tiered pricing to offer different levels of access, ensuring that all subscribers receive value for their investment without feeling pressured to upgrade unnecessarily.

Outcome: By maintaining a focus on ethical practices and clear communication, Casey Zander has successfully balanced profitability with integrity. His honest approach has built trust with his audience, leading to long-term subscriber loyalty and a positive reputation in the personal development space.

3. Renee Gracie (Former Racing Driver and Content Creator)

Background: Renee Gracie, a former racing driver, transitioned to content creation on OnlyFans, where she offers a mix of lifestyle content, behind-the-scenes insights, and personal vlogs. Renee's content strategy focuses on transparency and authenticity, while carefully managing her public image and personal boundaries.

Strategy: Renee Gracie has been successful in balancing profitability with ethical considerations by being upfront about the type of content she produces and the boundaries she maintains. She avoids explicit content, despite the potential financial rewards, and instead focuses on engaging her audience through personal stories, motivational content, and a candid look at her life post-racing.

Outcome: Renee's commitment to ethical content creation has allowed her to build a strong, supportive community that values her authenticity. Her approach has led to sustained profitability without compromising her values, proving that creators can succeed by staying true to their principles.

Practical Advice for Long-Term Sustainability and Integrity

1. Build a Sustainable Business Model: Creators should focus on building a business model that prioritizes long-term sustainability over short-term gains. This includes diversifying revenue streams, setting realistic goals, and avoiding practices that might offer immediate financial rewards but could damage reputation or integrity in the long run.

Advice: Evaluate your business model regularly to ensure it aligns with your values and long-term goals. Consider how different revenue streams contribute to your overall sustainability and make adjustments as needed to maintain a balance between profitability and ethical content creation.

2. Stay True to Your Brand and Values: Maintaining a consistent brand identity that aligns with your values is crucial for long-term success. Creators should resist the temptation to compromise their values for financial gain and instead focus on building a brand that reflects their true identity and resonates with their audience.

Advice: Regularly revisit your brand values and ensure that all content and interactions align with them. If faced with decisions that challenge your integrity, prioritize long-term brand health over short-term financial gain.

3. Engage in Continuous Learning and Adaptation: The digital content landscape is constantly evolving, and creators must stay informed about industry trends, audience preferences, and ethical practices. Continuous learning and adaptation help creators stay relevant and maintain their integrity while navigating new challenges and opportunities.

Advice: Invest in ongoing education, whether through formal courses, industry events, or self-directed learning. Stay connected with your audience to understand their changing needs and adapt your content strategy accordingly, all while upholding your ethical standards.

4. Foster a Supportive and Respectful Community: A supportive community is essential for long-term success. By fostering respect, inclusivity, and mutual support within your audience, you create a positive environment that encourages loyalty and organic growth.

Advice: Cultivate a community culture that reflects your values. Encourage positive interactions among subscribers, address issues promptly and fairly, and create content that reinforces the community's shared interests and goals.

5. Prioritize Mental Health and Well-being: Maintaining your own mental health and well-being is crucial for sustaining a successful content creation career. Setting boundaries, practicing self-care, and seeking support when needed are essential practices for long-term sustainability.

Advice: Schedule regular breaks, set clear boundaries around work and personal time, and don't hesitate to seek professional support if needed. Prioritizing your well-being helps you maintain the energy and creativity needed to produce high-quality content consistently.

Conclusion: Achieving Success Without Compromising Integrity

Balancing profitability with ethical considerations is both challenging and essential for long-term success in content creation. By implementing value-based pricing, diversifying income streams, and maintaining clear boundaries, creators can achieve their financial goals while staying true to their values. The experiences of successful creators demonstrate that it is possible to build a profitable and sustainable business without compromising integrity. By following best practices, engaging in continuous learning, and fostering a supportive community, creators can navigate the complexities of the digital content landscape while upholding ethical standards and achieving long-term success.

Community-Building and Positive Engagement

Importance of Building a Supportive and Respectful Community

1. Strengthening Subscriber Loyalty: Building a supportive and respectful community is essential for fostering long-term subscriber loyalty. When subscribers feel valued and part of a positive community, they are more likely to remain engaged with the content and continue their subscription. A strong community creates a sense of belonging, which enhances the overall experience and encourages subscribers to stay connected.

2. Enhancing Content Value: A positive community environment adds intrinsic value to the content being offered. Subscribers who engage in respectful and meaningful interactions with both the creator and fellow subscribers often derive additional satisfaction from their membership. This enhanced experience makes the content feel more valuable and justifies the cost of the subscription, leading to higher retention rates.

3. Promoting Word-of-Mouth Growth: A supportive community naturally encourages word-of-mouth promotion, as satisfied subscribers are more likely to recommend the content to friends and followers. This organic growth is one of the most effective forms of marketing, as it is driven by genuine enthusiasm and trust. A well-maintained community can become a powerful driver of new subscriptions and audience expansion.

4. Reducing Negative Interactions: Fostering a respectful community environment helps minimize negative interactions such as harassment, trolling, or toxic behavior. By setting clear expectations for conduct and actively moderating discussions, creators can maintain a positive atmosphere that encourages constructive and respectful communication. This not only protects the well-being of subscribers but also ensures a safer and more enjoyable space for everyone involved.

Techniques for Fostering Positive Interactions with Subscribers

1. Set Clear Community Guidelines: Establishing and communicating clear community guidelines is the foundation of positive engagement. These guidelines should outline acceptable behavior, expectations for interactions, and the consequences for violating the rules. By setting the tone early, creators can create a framework that supports respectful and constructive dialogue.

Example: A creator might post community guidelines at the top of their profile or in a pinned post, clearly stating that respectful communication is expected and that harassment or discrimination will not be tolerated. These guidelines serve as a reference point for all interactions within the community.

2. Encourage Active Participation: Creators can foster positive engagement by encouraging active participation from subscribers. This can be achieved through interactive content such as polls, Q&A sessions, and live streams, where subscribers have the opportunity to ask questions, share opinions, and engage directly with the creator. Encouraging subscribers to contribute ideas or feedback also makes them feel valued and involved in the content creation process.

Example: A creator could host a weekly Q&A session where subscribers submit questions in advance. During the live stream, the creator answers the most popular questions and discusses topics of interest to the community. This interactive format not only engages subscribers but also strengthens their connection to the creator.

3. Highlight and Reward Positive Behavior: Recognizing and rewarding positive behavior within the community reinforces the importance of respectful interactions. Creators can acknowledge subscribers who contribute constructively, show kindness, or support fellow community members. Rewards might include shoutouts, special content access, or other forms of recognition that highlight the subscriber's positive influence.

Example: A creator might run a "Subscriber of the Month" feature, where they highlight a subscriber who has been particularly supportive or engaged in the community. This recognition could include a shoutout in a video or a special mention in the creator's content, reinforcing the value of positive engagement.

4. Moderate Discussions Proactively: Active moderation is crucial for maintaining a positive community environment. Creators should regularly monitor discussions and intervene when necessary to address negative behavior or defuse potential conflicts. By addressing issues promptly and fairly, creators can prevent toxic behavior from spreading and ensure that the community remains a safe and welcoming space for all members.

Example: If a subscriber posts a comment that violates community guidelines, the creator (or a designated moderator) might privately message the subscriber to explain the issue and request that the comment be modified or removed. If necessary, the creator can take further action, such as muting or blocking the subscriber, to protect the community.

5. Foster Inclusivity and Diversity: Promoting inclusivity and diversity within the community ensures that all subscribers feel welcome and valued, regardless of their background, identity, or perspective. Creators can take steps to actively include diverse voices and perspectives in their content and discussions, creating a more enriching and supportive environment for everyone.

Example: A creator might celebrate cultural diversity by featuring content related to different traditions, holidays, or perspectives within their community. Additionally, they might create space for discussions on topics such as inclusion and equity, encouraging subscribers to share their experiences and insights in a respectful manner.

Role of Transparency and Authenticity in Community Relations

1. Building Trust Through Transparency: Transparency is a key component of building trust within a community. When creators are open about their content, pricing, and intentions, subscribers are more likely to feel secure in their support. Transparency also involves being honest about mistakes and taking responsibility when issues arise, which helps maintain credibility and trust.

Example: If a creator needs to change their content schedule or adjust subscription pricing, they might explain the reasons for the change in a detailed post or video. By sharing the context behind their decisions, the creator reassures subscribers that they are being considered and respected in the process.

2. Strengthening Connections with Authenticity: Authenticity is crucial for fostering deep and meaningful connections with subscribers. Creators who are genuine in their interactions and content are more likely to build a loyal and engaged community. Authenticity involves sharing one's true self, including personal stories, challenges, and successes, which helps subscribers relate to the creator on a human level.

Example: A creator might share a personal story about a challenge they've faced, such as overcoming a fear or pursuing a passion. By opening up about their experiences, the creator invites subscribers to connect with them on a deeper level, creating a more authentic and supportive community.

3. Encouraging Honest Feedback: Transparency and authenticity also involve encouraging honest feedback from subscribers. Creators who are open to receiving and acting on feedback demonstrate that they value their community's input and are committed to improving the subscriber experience. This feedback loop strengthens the community and helps creators stay aligned with their audience's needs and expectations.

Example: A creator might periodically ask subscribers for feedback on the content or community experience, either through surveys or direct messages. By actively seeking and responding to feedback, the creator shows that they are listening and willing to make changes to better serve their audience.

4. Consistency Between Words and Actions: Maintaining consistency between what a creator says and what they do is essential for building trust and credibility. Subscribers are more likely to respect and support creators who align their actions with their stated values and commitments. Consistency reinforces the authenticity of the creator and helps establish a reliable and trustworthy community dynamic.

Example: If a creator promises to produce content on a specific topic or to host a live event, following through on that promise is crucial for maintaining credibility. By consistently delivering on their commitments, the creator builds a reputation for reliability and integrity.

Conclusion: Creating a Positive and Engaged Community

Building a supportive and respectful community is essential for long-term success in content creation. By setting clear guidelines, encouraging active participation, and fostering inclusivity, creators can create a positive environment that enhances subscriber loyalty and satisfaction. Transparency and authenticity play a vital role in maintaining trust and deepening connections with the audience. By prioritizing these principles, creators can cultivate a thriving community that supports both their content and their values, leading to sustained growth and success in the digital content landscape.

8. Future of the OnlyFans Economy

Potential Regulatory Changes and Their Impact

1. Analysis of Proposed and Potential Regulations Affecting OnlyFans

Increased Financial Oversight: As platforms like OnlyFans continue to grow, there is a possibility of increased financial oversight from regulatory bodies. This could involve stricter reporting requirements for income earned on the platform, more rigorous tax compliance measures, and greater scrutiny of financial transactions to prevent money laundering and other illegal activities. Creators may be required to provide more detailed income reports and adhere to stricter tax regulations.

Example: In countries where digital earnings are becoming a significant part of the economy, governments might introduce specific tax codes or reporting requirements for income generated on platforms like OnlyFans. This could lead to additional administrative burdens for creators who may need to keep detailed financial records and possibly hire accountants to ensure compliance.

Content Moderation and Age Verification Laws: Another area of potential regulation is content moderation, particularly concerning explicit content and the protection of minors. Governments could impose stricter requirements for age verification, both for creators and subscribers, as well as more stringent rules on the type of content that can be legally shared on the platform. These regulations would likely focus on preventing underage access to explicit content and ensuring that all content is consensual and legal.

Example: If new laws mandate more comprehensive age verification processes, OnlyFans might need to implement advanced identity verification technologies. Creators could face delays in getting approved to publish content, and subscribers might be required to provide more detailed personal information before accessing certain types of content.

Data Privacy and Security Regulations: As concerns over data privacy and security continue to grow, OnlyFans and similar platforms could be subject to tighter regulations around how they handle user data. These regulations might require platforms to enhance their data protection measures, limit the amount of personal data they collect, and provide users with more control over their information. Creators and subscribers could be impacted by stricter privacy policies, potentially affecting how they interact on the platform.

Example: In response to new data privacy laws, OnlyFans might implement stricter data collection and storage practices, requiring more explicit consent from users before collecting or sharing data. Creators could be required to ensure that any third-party tools or services they use are compliant with these new regulations, adding complexity to their content management processes.

Anti-Pornography and Obscenity Laws: Some jurisdictions might pursue stricter anti-pornography and obscenity laws, which could directly impact the type of content allowed on OnlyFans. These laws could result in the platform being required to restrict or ban certain types of explicit content, particularly in conservative regions. Such regulations could lead to significant changes in the platform's content offerings and affect creators who primarily produce adult content.

Example: In regions where anti-pornography laws are enforced, OnlyFans might be required to implement content filters or block access to certain content types. Creators who rely on explicit content might need to adapt by focusing on non-explicit material or shifting their audience to regions where such restrictions do not apply.

2. Predictions for How Regulation Could Shape the Platform's Future

Content Diversification: In response to potential regulatory changes, it is likely that OnlyFans will see a diversification of content types. Creators might shift their focus away from explicit content to avoid legal complications, exploring other forms of digital content such as fitness, education, lifestyle, or entertainment. This diversification could broaden the platform's appeal to a wider audience and reduce its reliance on adult content.

Example: A creator who primarily produces adult content might start offering fitness tutorials, wellness advice, or cooking classes as a way to diversify their income and mitigate the risks associated with stricter content regulations.

Stricter Platform Policies and Increased Compliance Costs: As regulatory pressures increase, OnlyFans may need to implement stricter platform policies to ensure compliance with new laws. This could include more rigorous content review processes, enhanced user verification, and greater transparency in financial transactions. These changes could lead to increased compliance costs for both the platform and creators, potentially resulting in higher fees or reduced payouts for creators.

Example: OnlyFans might introduce a new content approval process that requires creators to submit their material for review before publication. While this could help ensure compliance with legal standards, it might also slow down content production and add to the workload for creators.

Shift Toward Professionalization: With increased regulation, there may be a shift toward the professionalization of content creation on platforms like OnlyFans. Creators who treat their work as a business, investing in legal advice, financial planning, and professional content production, are likely to be better positioned to navigate regulatory changes. This professionalization could raise the bar for content quality and set new standards for success on the platform.

Example: A creator who anticipates regulatory changes might proactively seek legal counsel to ensure their content complies with potential new laws. They might also invest in high-quality production equipment and professional editing services to elevate their content, appealing to a broader, more discerning audience.

Regional Variations in Platform Access: As different regions implement varying regulations, OnlyFans might need to adapt its services to comply with local laws. This could lead to regional variations in the platform's content offerings, accessibility, and user experience. Creators may need to tailor their content or marketing strategies based on the regulations and audience preferences in different regions.

Example: In a country with strict content regulations, OnlyFans might offer a localized version of the platform that limits certain types of content or features. Creators targeting audiences in that region might need to adjust their content strategies accordingly, focusing on non-explicit material or culturally relevant content.

3. Strategies for Creators to Adapt to Regulatory Changes

Stay Informed and Proactive: Creators should stay informed about potential regulatory changes and actively monitor developments in relevant laws and policies. By staying ahead of the curve, creators can anticipate changes and take proactive steps to ensure compliance. This might involve participating in industry discussions, following legal news, and consulting with legal professionals who specialize in digital content.

Example: A creator might subscribe to newsletters or join online forums focused on digital content law to stay updated on potential regulatory changes. By keeping informed, they can adapt their content and business practices before new regulations take effect.

Diversify Content and Revenue Streams: To mitigate the impact of regulatory changes, creators should consider diversifying their content and revenue streams. This might involve expanding into new content areas, exploring alternative platforms, or developing additional income sources such as merchandise, affiliate marketing, or sponsored content. Diversification helps reduce dependence on a single platform or content type, making creators more resilient to regulatory shifts.

Example: A creator who primarily produces adult content might start a podcast on a related topic, such as relationships or sexual health, to reach a broader audience and create an additional revenue stream that is less vulnerable to content restrictions.

Invest in Legal and Financial Advice: As regulations become more complex, creators should consider investing in legal and financial advice to navigate the new landscape. Consulting with professionals who understand the legalities of digital content creation can help creators avoid potential pitfalls and ensure that their business practices are compliant with evolving laws. Financial advice can also help creators manage increased compliance costs and optimize their revenue strategies.

Example: A creator might hire a lawyer to review their content and business practices, ensuring that they comply with new regulations. They could also work with a financial advisor to create a budget that accounts for potential increases in platform fees or legal expenses.

Develop a Strong Personal Brand: Building a strong personal brand can help creators remain successful even in the face of regulatory changes. A well-established brand that resonates with a loyal audience can help creators retain subscribers and attract new followers, even if they need to shift their content focus. A strong brand also opens up opportunities for partnerships, sponsorships, and other forms of monetization that are less dependent on platform-specific content rules.

Example: A creator might focus on developing a consistent visual style, tone, and message across all their content and platforms, building a brand that stands out and attracts a dedicated audience. By cultivating a strong brand, the creator can more easily transition to new content types or platforms if necessary.

Leverage Alternative Platforms and Technologies: In response to stricter regulations on platforms like OnlyFans, creators might explore alternative platforms or technologies that offer more flexibility or are less heavily regulated. Decentralized platforms, blockchain-based content distribution, or niche content platforms could provide opportunities for creators to continue their work without the same level of regulatory constraints.

Example: A creator facing new content restrictions on OnlyFans might start using a decentralized platform that allows for greater content freedom. By diversifying their presence across multiple platforms, the creator reduces their dependence on any single site and gains more control over their content.

Conclusion: Navigating the Future of the OnlyFans Economy

The future of the OnlyFans economy is likely to be shaped by a range of potential regulatory changes that will impact both the platform and its creators. By staying informed, diversifying content and revenue streams, and investing in legal and financial advice, creators can adapt to these changes while maintaining their profitability and integrity. Building a strong personal brand and exploring alternative platforms can also help creators navigate the evolving digital content landscape. As the industry continues to evolve, creators who proactively adjust to regulatory shifts will be best positioned to thrive in the changing OnlyFans economy.

Predictions for the Platform's Evolution

Trends and Innovations Likely to Shape OnlyFans' Future

1. Diversification of Content Beyond Adult Entertainment: As regulatory scrutiny increases and societal attitudes toward digital content evolve, OnlyFans is likely to continue diversifying its content offerings beyond adult entertainment. The platform has already seen growth in areas such as fitness, cooking, music, and education, and this trend is expected to accelerate. By expanding into these and other niches, OnlyFans can attract a broader audience and reduce its dependence on explicit content, making the platform more sustainable in the long term.

Example: Creators specializing in personal development, mental health, or entrepreneurship might increasingly find success on OnlyFans, offering exclusive content such as workshops, courses, and one-on-one coaching sessions. This shift could also attract a more diverse subscriber base, including professionals seeking educational or inspirational content.

2. Integration of Emerging Technologies: To stay competitive and meet the evolving needs of its users, OnlyFans may integrate emerging technologies such as augmented reality (AR), virtual reality (VR), and blockchain. These innovations could enhance the user experience by offering more immersive content and new ways to interact with creators. For instance, AR and VR could allow subscribers to participate in virtual events or experience content in a more interactive and engaging way.

Example: A fitness creator might use AR technology to create a virtual workout environment where subscribers can follow along with exercises in a more immersive setting. Alternatively, a music artist could host a VR concert, allowing fans to experience the performance as if they were attending in person.

3. Expansion of Creator Tools and Analytics: To support creators in growing their businesses, OnlyFans is likely to develop more advanced tools and analytics. These features could include enhanced content management systems, deeper insights into subscriber behavior, and improved marketing tools. By providing creators with better data and resources, OnlyFans can help them optimize their content strategies, increase engagement, and maximize earnings.

Example: OnlyFans might introduce a suite of analytics tools that allow creators to track the performance of their content in real-time, identify trends in subscriber preferences, and tailor their offerings to meet demand more effectively. Additionally, the platform could offer automated marketing tools that help creators promote their content across social media and other channels.

4. Increased Emphasis on Community Building: As the platform continues to evolve, there will likely be a greater emphasis on community building and fostering positive interactions between creators and subscribers. This could include the introduction of new features that facilitate group interactions, such as forums, community challenges, or collaborative content creation. By focusing on community, OnlyFans can enhance subscriber loyalty and create a more vibrant and engaged user base.

Example: OnlyFans might launch community-specific features where subscribers can participate in group discussions, share content related to the creator's niche, or collaborate on projects. For example, a cooking influencer could host a weekly recipe challenge where subscribers cook the same dish and share their results, fostering a sense of camaraderie and interaction.

5. Focus on Sustainability and Ethical Practices: In response to growing concerns about digital content ethics, OnlyFans is likely to place a stronger focus on sustainability and ethical practices. This could involve implementing stricter guidelines for content creation, offering resources for creators to manage their mental health, and promoting fair pricing models. Emphasizing ethics and sustainability will be crucial for maintaining the platform's reputation and ensuring long-term success.

Example: OnlyFans could introduce a Creator Well-being Program that provides mental health support, ethical content creation workshops, and resources for managing the pressures of online fame. Additionally, the platform might promote campaigns that encourage creators to adopt sustainable practices, such as minimizing digital carbon footprints or supporting social causes.

Potential New Features and Business Models

1. Subscription Bundling and Loyalty Programs: To incentivize long-term subscriptions and increase revenue, OnlyFans might introduce subscription bundling and loyalty programs. Subscription bundling would allow users to subscribe to multiple creators at a discounted rate, encouraging them to explore more content on the platform. Loyalty programs could reward subscribers for their continued support with perks such as exclusive content, early access, or discounts on merchandise.

Example: A user interested in fitness and wellness content might purchase a bundle that includes subscriptions to multiple fitness creators, a yoga instructor, and a nutrition coach. In return, they receive a discount on the overall cost and access to a members-only wellness community.

2. Pay-Per-Experience Features: In addition to the traditional subscription model, OnlyFans could introduce pay-per-experience features that offer unique, one-time events or content. This could include virtual meet-and-greets, personalized video messages, live workshops, or special event access. By offering exclusive, high-value experiences, creators can generate additional income while providing something truly special for their fans.

Example: A popular musician on OnlyFans might offer a limited number of virtual backstage passes for an upcoming concert, where fans can interact with the artist, ask questions, and receive personalized shoutouts. This pay-per-experience feature could command a premium price, appealing to the most dedicated fans.

3. Creator Collaborations and Cross-Promotions: OnlyFans might further develop features that facilitate collaborations between creators, allowing them to co-create content and cross-promote each other's work. These collaborations could be highlighted through dedicated sections of the platform or featured content, helping creators reach new audiences and create synergistic partnerships.

Example: Two creators from different niches—such as a fitness instructor and a nutritionist—might collaborate on a joint health challenge, offering subscribers a comprehensive package that includes workouts, meal plans, and wellness tips. This collaboration could be promoted through a special feature on the platform, attracting subscribers from both creators' audiences.

4. Marketplace for Digital Products and Services: To diversify revenue streams, OnlyFans could launch a marketplace where creators can sell digital products and services, such as eBooks, courses, digital art, or personalized consultations. This marketplace would allow creators to monetize their expertise beyond traditional content, providing subscribers with additional ways to engage with and learn from their favorite creators.

Example: A content creator who specializes in photography might offer an eBook on advanced photography techniques, alongside online workshops and personalized photo critiques. Subscribers could purchase these products directly through the OnlyFans marketplace, expanding the creator's income sources.

5. Enhanced Privacy and Security Features: As privacy and security remain top concerns for users, OnlyFans may introduce enhanced features to protect both creators and subscribers. This could include more robust privacy controls, such as anonymous browsing options for subscribers, advanced content watermarking to prevent unauthorized distribution, and two-factor authentication for account security.

Example: OnlyFans might offer a "ghost mode" feature for subscribers, allowing them to browse content and interact with creators anonymously. For creators, the platform could implement a new watermarking system that tracks content leaks and assists in identifying and taking down pirated material.

Implications for Creators, Subscribers, and the Broader Digital Economy

1. Empowerment of Creators: The continued evolution of OnlyFans is likely to further empower creators by providing them with more tools, insights, and opportunities to monetize their content. As the platform diversifies and introduces new features, creators will have more ways to engage with their audience, expand their brand, and build sustainable businesses. This empowerment could lead to a shift in how content creators operate, with more focus on professionalization and long-term strategy.

Example: Creators who adapt to new features like advanced analytics or digital marketplaces will be better positioned to grow their income and influence. This professionalization could lead to the emergence of creator-driven micro-economies, where influencers manage complex, multi-channel content businesses.

2. Enhanced Subscriber Experience: For subscribers, the evolution of OnlyFans promises a more personalized, immersive, and engaging experience. New features like AR/VR content, pay-per-experience options, and community-driven interactions will allow subscribers to connect with creators in deeper and more meaningful ways. This could lead to increased subscriber satisfaction and loyalty, driving further growth for the platform.

Example: Subscribers might enjoy a more tailored experience where they can choose from a variety of content types and engagement levels, from interactive AR fitness classes to exclusive one-on-one consultations. The diversity of options will make the platform more appealing to a broader audience.

3. Broader Impact on the Digital Economy: As OnlyFans continues to evolve, it will have a broader impact on the digital economy by influencing how content is created, consumed, and monetized. The platform's success could inspire similar models across different industries, leading to the growth of creator-centric platforms that prioritize direct audience engagement and diversified revenue streams. Additionally, OnlyFans' innovations in privacy, security, and community-building could set new standards for digital content platforms.

Example: The success of OnlyFans might encourage other platforms, such as Patreon or YouTube, to adopt similar features or business models. This could lead to a more competitive landscape where content creators have multiple platforms to choose from, each offering unique tools and opportunities for monetization.

Conclusion: Preparing for the Future of OnlyFans

The future of OnlyFans is likely to be shaped by trends and innovations that diversify content, enhance creator tools, and improve subscriber experiences. As the platform evolves, creators and subscribers will need to adapt to new features and business models that offer more opportunities for engagement and monetization. The broader digital economy will also feel the impact of OnlyFans' innovations, potentially leading to new standards and practices across the industry. By staying informed and proactive, creators can position themselves to thrive in this dynamic and rapidly changing environment, ensuring long-term success on the platform.

Long-Term Societal and Economic Implications

Forecasting the Broader Impact of OnlyFans on Society and the Economy

1. Shifting Labor Dynamics in the Gig Economy: OnlyFans represents a significant evolution in the gig economy, where individuals can monetize their personal brands and content directly to their audience. As platforms like OnlyFans continue to grow, we may see a shift in labor dynamics, with more people pursuing content creation as a primary or supplementary income source. This trend could lead to the redefinition of traditional employment structures, where individuals increasingly rely on multiple income streams from various digital platforms.

Example: A person working part-time in retail might supplement their income by creating content on OnlyFans, leading to a more diversified and flexible income structure. As more people adopt this model, the gig economy could expand further, with content creation becoming a viable alternative to traditional employment for many.

2. Economic Empowerment and Entrepreneurial Opportunities: OnlyFans has the potential to economically empower creators by providing them with a platform to directly monetize their skills, creativity, and influence. This empowerment could lead to an increase in entrepreneurial activity, particularly among marginalized groups who may face barriers in traditional job markets. By enabling individuals to build their own businesses and control their financial futures, OnlyFans could contribute to a broader democratization of economic opportunities.

Example: A creator from a traditionally underrepresented community might use OnlyFans to share cultural content, educational resources, or personal stories, building a business that supports themselves and their community. This entrepreneurial activity not only provides financial independence but also helps diversify the content available online.

3. Influence on Consumer Behavior and Content Consumption: As OnlyFans and similar platforms grow, consumer behavior and content consumption patterns are likely to shift. The demand for personalized, exclusive content will continue to rise, leading consumers to prioritize direct interactions with creators over passive consumption of mass media. This shift could challenge traditional media companies, pushing them to adapt by offering more interactive and user-driven content experiences.

Example: Subscribers might increasingly prefer spending money on personalized experiences, such as live Q&A sessions or custom content, rather than on traditional media subscriptions like cable TV. This change in consumer preferences could lead to a decline in traditional media consumption and a rise in direct-to-consumer content platforms.

4. Impacts on Mental Health and Well-being: The rise of platforms like OnlyFans could have complex implications for mental health and well-being, both for creators and consumers. While the platform offers creators financial independence and the ability to express themselves creatively, it also introduces challenges such as maintaining personal boundaries, dealing with online harassment, and managing the pressures of content production. For subscribers, the platform may foster both positive community interactions and unhealthy parasocial relationships, depending on how they engage with content.

Example: A creator might experience burnout due to the constant pressure to produce new content and maintain engagement with subscribers. On the other hand, a subscriber who forms a parasocial relationship with a creator might struggle with unrealistic expectations or emotional dependency. These scenarios highlight the need for mental health support and awareness in the digital content space.

Role of OnlyFans in the Future of Digital Content and Social Media

1. Leading the Trend Toward Creator-Centric Platforms: OnlyFans has positioned itself as a pioneer in the creator-centric platform model, where individual content creators have direct control over their revenue and audience engagement. This trend is likely to influence the broader social media landscape, with other platforms adopting similar models that prioritize creator autonomy and direct monetization. As a result, we may see a decline in traditional ad-driven social media platforms in favor of those that allow for more direct creator-consumer interactions.

Example: Platforms like Instagram or YouTube might introduce new features that allow creators to offer subscription-based content or personalized interactions, following the model popularized by OnlyFans. This shift would empower creators to monetize their influence more effectively, reducing their reliance on advertising revenue.

2. Expanding the Definition of Digital Content: The success of OnlyFans is likely to broaden the definition of digital content, encompassing a wider range of experiences, from educational courses and fitness training to virtual events and personalized services. As the platform continues to diversify its offerings, other content platforms may follow suit, leading to a more inclusive and varied digital content ecosystem that caters to niche interests and personalized experiences.

Example: A creator on OnlyFans might offer a combination of digital art tutorials, virtual gallery tours, and personalized critiques, expanding the notion of what constitutes valuable digital content. This diversified approach could inspire other platforms to support more varied and specialized content offerings.

3. Driving Innovation in Content Monetization: OnlyFans is likely to continue driving innovation in content monetization strategies, influencing how creators and platforms think about revenue generation. The platform's success could lead to the development of new monetization tools, such as microtransactions, tiered subscriptions, and pay-per-experience models, which could be adopted across the digital content industry. These innovations would give creators more flexibility in how they monetize their work and interact with their audience.

Example: OnlyFans might introduce a new microtransaction system that allows subscribers to tip creators for specific content pieces or interactions, enabling creators to generate additional income from smaller, more frequent transactions. This model could be replicated by other platforms, further diversifying monetization options for creators.

Ethical and Cultural Considerations for the Platform's Continued Growth

1. Navigating the Ethics of Content Creation and Monetization: As OnlyFans grows, the platform will need to address the ethical implications of content creation and monetization, particularly concerning issues like consent, privacy, and exploitation. Ensuring that creators have the tools and resources to protect their rights and well-being will be crucial for maintaining the platform's reputation and fostering a positive content ecosystem. This might involve implementing stricter content guidelines, offering mental health support, and providing clear channels for reporting and resolving disputes.

Example: OnlyFans could introduce a comprehensive support program for creators, including access to mental health professionals, legal advice, and educational resources on ethical content creation. By proactively addressing these concerns, the platform can help creators navigate the challenges of digital content production while maintaining ethical standards.

2. Addressing Cultural and Societal Impacts: The rise of OnlyFans has significant cultural and societal implications, particularly regarding the normalization of adult content and the changing dynamics of online relationships. As the platform continues to grow, it will need to consider its impact on societal norms and values, particularly concerning issues like gender dynamics, body image, and the commodification of intimacy. Engaging in open dialogue with stakeholders, including creators, subscribers, and advocacy groups, will be essential for navigating these complex issues.

Example: OnlyFans might partner with cultural and academic institutions to explore the societal impacts of its platform, hosting discussions and research initiatives that examine how digital content creation is shaping cultural norms. By fostering these conversations, OnlyFans can contribute to a more informed and balanced understanding of its role in society.

3. Promoting Inclusivity and Diversity: Ensuring that OnlyFans remains an inclusive and diverse platform will be key to its continued growth. This involves actively supporting creators from underrepresented communities, promoting diverse content types, and fostering an environment where all voices can be heard. Inclusivity and diversity not only enrich the platform's content offerings but also contribute to a more equitable digital economy.

Example: OnlyFans could launch initiatives that spotlight creators from diverse backgrounds, offering grants, mentorship programs, or promotional support to help them grow their audience. These efforts would not only support individual creators but also enhance the platform's overall diversity and appeal.

4. Balancing Profitability with Ethical Responsibility: As OnlyFans continues to grow, it will face the challenge of balancing profitability with ethical responsibility. This includes ensuring that monetization strategies do not exploit creators or subscribers, that content policies are enforced fairly and transparently, and that the platform remains committed to supporting the well-being of its community. Striking this balance will be crucial for maintaining the platform's long-term sustainability and reputation.

Example: OnlyFans might implement a profit-sharing model where a percentage of platform revenue is reinvested into creator support programs, such as legal aid, educational resources, and mental health services. This approach would align the platform's financial success with the well-being of its creators, fostering a more sustainable and ethical business model.

Conclusion: Preparing for the Societal and Economic Impact of OnlyFans

The long-term societal and economic implications of OnlyFans are profound, influencing everything from labor dynamics and consumer behavior to cultural norms and ethical standards. As the platform continues to evolve, it will play a pivotal role in shaping the future of digital content and social media. By addressing ethical and cultural considerations, promoting inclusivity, and balancing profitability with responsibility, OnlyFans can position itself as a leader in the digital economy, setting new standards for how content is created, consumed, and monetized. Creators, subscribers, and the broader society will need to engage in ongoing dialogue to navigate these changes and ensure that the platform's growth contributes positively to the digital landscape.

9. Conclusion

As we reach the conclusion of this exploration into the complex and rapidly evolving world of OnlyFans, it is essential to reflect on the broader implications of the platform, not just for those who participate directly, but for society as a whole. OnlyFans, and platforms like it, have fundamentally reshaped the way we think about content creation, personal branding, and the digital economy. However, with these opportunities come profound moral and ethical considerations that we must address as a collective society.

Final Message to the Reader

The central message of this book is that OnlyFans is more than just a platform for content distribution; it is a microcosm of the broader shifts occurring in our digital society. It represents the democratization of content creation, where anyone with internet access can build an audience, monetize their talents, and achieve financial independence. But with this power comes responsibility—both for creators who produce content and for subscribers who consume it.

As a reader, you are encouraged to think critically about the role of digital platforms in your life and the lives of others. The decisions we make as consumers, creators, and members of society have far-reaching consequences that extend beyond the screen. It is our collective responsibility to ensure that these platforms evolve in ways that are ethical, inclusive, and respectful of the dignity of all individuals involved.

Moral and Ethical Implications

The rise of OnlyFans has brought to the forefront critical moral and ethical questions that touch on issues of identity, autonomy, and societal values. For creators, especially women, the platform offers a means of financial empowerment and self-expression, but it also presents challenges that are deeply intertwined with societal expectations and gender norms.

Impact on Women: For many women, OnlyFans has been a double-edged sword. On one hand, it provides an unprecedented level of control over their content and income, allowing them to break free from traditional employment constraints and societal expectations. On the other hand, the platform can exacerbate the pressures to conform to narrow standards of beauty and sexuality, sometimes leading to moral conflicts and societal judgment. The commodification of personal and intimate aspects of one's life can have lasting effects on self-perception and societal reputation, making it essential for creators to navigate these waters carefully.

Impact on Men: For men, the platform often presents a different set of moral challenges. The increasing normalization of paying for personalized, intimate content can blur the lines between healthy admiration and unhealthy obsession. The transactional nature of relationships on the platform can distort perceptions of intimacy and human connection, leading to potential emotional and psychological consequences. It is crucial for men to approach these interactions with awareness and respect, understanding the complex dynamics at play.

Societal Impact

Beyond the individual experiences of creators and subscribers, OnlyFans has broader societal implications that cannot be ignored. It challenges traditional norms around labor, gender, and media consumption, pushing society to reconsider what is acceptable in the digital age. As the platform continues to grow, it will play a pivotal role in shaping the future of digital content, influencing everything from economic models to cultural norms.

Economic Empowerment and the Digital Economy: OnlyFans has demonstrated the potential for digital platforms to empower individuals economically, particularly those who may have been marginalized or overlooked by traditional industries. By providing a space for diverse voices and content types, the platform contributes to the democratization of economic opportunities. However, this also means that society must grapple with the ethical implications of this new digital economy, ensuring that it remains a space of empowerment rather than exploitation.

Cultural Shifts and Ethical Responsibility: As OnlyFans continues to influence cultural norms, it is essential to maintain an ongoing dialogue about the ethical responsibilities of both the platform and its users. Society must work together to establish norms that protect the well-being of creators and consumers alike, promoting a culture of respect, transparency, and ethical behavior. The decisions made today will shape the future of digital interaction, making it crucial to prioritize values that support long-term societal health and well-being.

Conclusion

In conclusion, OnlyFans is a powerful example of how digital platforms can transform lives, economies, and societies. But with this transformation comes the need for careful consideration of the moral and ethical implications. As creators, subscribers, and members of a global society, we must strive to engage with these platforms in ways that are respectful, responsible, and reflective of our shared values.

As you close this book, I encourage you to think deeply about your role in this evolving digital landscape. Whether you are a content creator, a subscriber, or simply a curious observer, your actions and decisions contribute to the shaping of this new digital frontier. Let us work together to ensure that the future of digital content is one that empowers individuals, upholds ethical standards, and enriches society as a whole.

Acknowledgments

I am deeply grateful to everyone who has supported me in the creation and publication of this book.

To my family, whose unwavering encouragement and belief in my work have been a constant source of inspiration, thank you for standing by me every step of the way.

I extend my heartfelt appreciation to my friends and colleagues who provided valuable insights, feedback, and moral support throughout the writing process. Your contributions have enriched this book beyond measure.

I am indebted to the experts and professionals who generously shared their knowledge and expertise, contributing to the depth and accuracy of the content presented in these pages.

Special thanks to kevin, whose guidance and encouragement have been instrumental in shaping the ideas and structure of this book.

I would also like to express my gratitude to the individuals who assisted with editing, formatting, and designing the book, ensuring its professional presentation.

Lastly, I dedicate this book to my readers. Your interest in exploring and understanding the complexities of relationships motivates me to continue sharing insights and knowledge.

Thank you all for being a part of this incredible journey of self-publishing.

Appendix

This appendix serves as a resource for further exploration of the topics covered in the book, offering additional insights, references, and tools that readers can use to deepen their understanding of the OnlyFans platform and its broader implications on society, the economy, and digital content creation.

A. Additional Reading and Resources

1. Books on Digital Content Creation and the Gig Economy:

○ *The Gig Economy: The Complete Guide to Getting Better Work, Taking More Time Off, and Financing the Life You Want* by Diane Mulcahy

○ *Hustle and Gig: Struggling and Surviving in the Sharing Economy* by Alexandrea J. Ravenelle

○ *The Future of Work: Robots, AI, and Automation* by Darrell M. West

○ *Superfans: The Easy Way to Stand Out, Grow Your Tribe, and Build a Successful Business* by Pat Flynn

2. Articles and Academic Papers on Ethical Considerations in Digital Platforms:

○ "The Ethics of Content Moderation on Social Media Platforms" by Tarleton Gillespie, *Social Media + Society* (2018)

○ "Digital Labour and Development: Impacts of Global Digital Platforms on Work and Workers" by Mark Graham et al., *International Development Planning Review* (2020)

○ "The Commodification of Intimacy in the Digital Age" by Illana Gershon, *American Ethnologist* (2011)

○ "Privacy, Ethics, and the Digital Age: A Closer Look at Online Content Creation" by Sarah Roberts, *Journal of Information Ethics* (2019)

3. Websites and Platforms for Content Creators:

○ *Patreon*: A platform similar to OnlyFans, allowing creators to offer exclusive content to their supporters.

○ *Teachable*: A platform for creating and selling online courses, suitable for creators looking to expand their offerings.

○ *Skillshare*: A platform where creators can teach and share their skills through online classes.

4. Mental Health Resources for Content Creators:

○ *Therapy for Creators*: A network of therapists specializing in issues faced by digital content creators.

○ *The Trevor Project*: Provides mental health resources and support for LGBTQ+ individuals, including those involved in digital content creation.

○ *Calm*: A meditation and mental wellness app that can help creators manage stress and maintain balance.

B. Glossary of Terms

1. **OnlyFans:** A subscription-based social media platform that allows creators to share content directly with their subscribers, often involving personalized interactions or exclusive material.

2. **Parasocial Relationships:** One-sided relationships where one party (often a fan or subscriber) feels a deep connection to another party (often a creator or celebrity) who may be unaware of their existence.

3. **Gig Economy:** An economic model in which individuals work independently, often on short-term contracts or freelance jobs, rather than traditional full-time employment.

4. **Digital Content Creation:** The process of producing content (such as videos, articles, or art) for distribution and monetization through digital platforms.

5. **Monetization:** The process of generating revenue from content, often through subscriptions, advertisements, sponsorships, or sales of digital products.

6. **Commodification:** The process of turning something into a commodity that can be bought and sold, often leading to the commercialization of personal or intimate aspects of life.

7. **Ethical Content Creation:** The practice of producing digital content in a way that respects the rights, dignity, and well-being of both the creator and the audience, adhering to ethical standards and norms.

C. Frequently Asked Questions (FAQs)

1. How can creators balance profitability with ethical considerations on platforms like OnlyFans?

- Creators can balance profitability with ethics by setting clear personal boundaries, being transparent with their audience, and diversifying their income streams to reduce pressure. Additionally, staying informed about platform policies and industry trends can help creators make decisions that align with their values.

2. What are the potential long-term impacts of OnlyFans on society?

- The long-term impacts of OnlyFans include shifts in labor dynamics, changes in consumer behavior, and challenges to traditional norms around gender, relationships, and media consumption. As the platform continues to grow, it will likely influence how we think about work, intimacy, and economic empowerment in the digital age.

3. How can subscribers engage with content on OnlyFans in a healthy and respectful way?

- Subscribers can engage healthily by setting clear boundaries, being mindful of the transactional nature of the platform, and respecting the creators' personal and professional limits. It's also important for subscribers to recognize the difference between supportive engagement and unhealthy attachment.

4. What role does OnlyFans play in the broader digital economy?

- OnlyFans is a significant player in the digital economy, offering a model of direct-to-consumer monetization that empowers creators to generate income independently. Its success has implications for the future of work, content creation, and how individuals can leverage digital platforms for economic empowerment.

D. Tools for Content Creators

1. Content Planning Templates:

○ Templates that help creators plan their content schedule, including ideas for diversification and strategies for maintaining consistency and quality.

2. Revenue Tracking Spreadsheets:

○ Tools for tracking income from various revenue streams, helping creators manage their finances and plan for sustainable growth.

3. Social Media Management Tools:

○ Software like Hootsuite or Buffer that assists creators in managing their social media presence, scheduling posts, and engaging with their audience across platforms.

4. Legal Resources:

○ Access to templates for contracts, content rights agreements, and other legal documents that creators might need to protect their work and ensure compliance with platform policies.

E. Case Studies of Successful Content Creators

1. Case Study 1: From Fitness Instructor to Digital Entrepreneur

o A fitness instructor who used OnlyFans to transition from in-person training to digital content creation, expanding their brand and income streams through online workouts, nutritional guides, and personalized coaching.

2. Case Study 2: Navigating the Challenges of Adult Content Creation

o A creator who successfully built a career in adult content on OnlyFans while navigating the ethical and personal challenges of the industry, including managing public perception and ensuring long-term financial stability.

3. Case Study 3: Leveraging OnlyFans for Educational Content

o An educator who found success on OnlyFans by offering niche courses and workshops on topics not covered in traditional educational settings, demonstrating the platform's potential beyond adult entertainment.

F. Ethical Considerations Checklist for Creators

- **Transparency:** Am I being honest with my audience about what they can expect from my content?

- **Boundaries:** Have I set and communicated clear boundaries regarding the type of content I will produce and the interactions I will engage in?

- **Privacy:** Am I protecting my privacy and that of my subscribers?

- **Inclusivity:** Is my content inclusive and respectful of diverse perspectives and experiences?

- **Sustainability:** Am I creating content in a way that is sustainable for my mental and emotional well-being?

G. Future Trends in Digital Content Creation

- **Immersive Experiences:** The rise of AR and VR in content creation, offering subscribers more interactive and engaging experiences.

- **Decentralized Platforms:** The potential for blockchain-based platforms to offer creators greater control over their content and revenue.

- **Ethical AI:** The role of artificial intelligence in content creation and moderation, and the ethical considerations involved in its use.

- **Micro-Monetization:** Emerging models for monetizing smaller interactions, such as tipping or microtransactions, that allow creators to generate income from a broader range of content.

H. Legal and Regulatory Considerations

- **Understanding Platform Policies:** Key points of platform terms of service and content guidelines that creators need to be aware of.

● **Tax Obligations:** Information on managing taxes as a digital content creator, including tips on tracking income and expenses.

● **Intellectual Property:** Protecting your content from unauthorized use and understanding your rights as a creator.